A Guide
to
Student Teaching
in Music

A Guide to Student Teaching in Music

JOAN BONEY / LOIS RHEA

Meadows School of the Arts
Southern Methodist University
Dallas, Texas

PRENTICE-HALL, INC., Englewood Cliffs, New Jersey

Printed in the United States of America

C–13-370718-0
P–13-370692-3

Library of Congress Catalog Card No.: 79-95749

Current Printing (last digit):

10 9 8 7 6 5 4 3

PRENTICE-HALL INTERNATIONAL, INC., London
PRENTICE-HALL OF AUSTRALIA, PTY. LTD., Sydney
PRENTICE-HALL OF CANADA, LTD., Toronto
PRENTICE-HALL OF INDIA PRIVATE LTD., New Delhi
PRENTICE-HALL OF JAPAN, INC., Tokyo

Preface

To the Student Teacher

This book has been written for the purpose of helping you bridge a gap between pedagogical theory and classroom teaching. It is recommended that the book be used along with the materials given to you in your music methods courses. Ideally, you will have read all of the content of this book before you begin student teaching. If this is the case, the book will remain in your personal library as a reference during your tenure as a teacher.

Although portions of the book are related to specific areas of music teaching, we recommend that the student teacher read each chapter, thereby increasing his understanding of the total music program.

In composing this material we gratefully acknowledge the following persons: Mrs. Patricia Bond, Mr. M. Browning Combs, Miss Charlotte DuBois, Mrs. Doris Griffith, Mr. Edward Hamilton, Miss Rosemary Heffley, Miss Zelwanda Hendrick, Dr. W. Henry Kennedy, Dr. David McGuire, Dr. Jack Roberts, Dr. Travis Shelton, and Mr. Weldon Wendland.

Joan Boney
Lois Rhea

Contents

4

PLANNING AND TEACHING: CHORAL MUSIC 33

Organization of the Rehearsal
Presentation
Elementary School Choir
Junior High School Choir
Senior High School Choir
Evaluation

5

PLANNING AND TEACHING: GENERAL MUSIC 48

Organizing Materials
Lesson Planning
Elementary (Lower) School: Lesson Plans
Secondary School: Lesson Plans
Presentation
Elementary School Presentation
Secondary School Presentation
Evaluation

6

THE ORGANIZATION AND DEVELOPMENT
OF THE PERFORMING GROUP 64

Recruitment of Students
Developing a Theory of Recruitment
Recruitment Techniques
Patron Organizations
Budget and Fund Raising
Uniforms
Selecting the Uniform
Manufacture of the Uniform
Financing the Uniforms
Maintenance of Uniforms
Publicity
Purposes of Publicity

1

Introduction to Student Teaching in Music

The student teaching experience provides an opportunity to observe and to work actively in various aspects of the music teaching field. Rather than being a terminal course in your college curriculum, student teaching marks the beginning of your career. Given the proper equipment—musical skills, methodology, and an understanding of human relations—you will find student teaching to be one of the most challenging and rewarding experiences of college life.

Although student teaching is designed to give you an opportunity to learn by doing, it is unlike other on-the-job experiences. For example, if an apprentice secretary makes a mistake while typing a letter, she can erase the error. The secretary is dealing with objects while the student teacher works with people. Consequently, as a student teacher you must proceed with a type of cautious daring. You must be allowed, within certain boundaries, to try out pedagogical theories, but you must never lose sight of the responsibility that is yours in guiding the musical growth of your students.

The suggestions discussed herewith constitute an effort to help you to understand the purpose of the student teaching program and the role of those persons with whom you will be associated.

Goals of Student Teaching

The following statements should provide an understanding of some of the goals of student teaching in music:

1. Student teaching should give you insight into the total school program.
2. Student teaching should provide the opportunity whereby you can apply, through teaching, the knowledge and musical skills acquired during your earlier training.
3. Student teaching should help you to gain confidence in yourself as a teacher through planning, teaching, and evaluating.

4. Student teaching should foster a professional attitude and a desire for professional growth.
5. Student teaching should provide insights into the fundamental differences between the processes of learning for oneself and that of teaching others.

Through periodic review and consideration of the goals of student teaching, you may determine your growth. Your college supervisor and cooperating teacher will be of assistance in helping you to reach these goals.

Activities of Student Teaching

The activities of the student teaching term are generally divided into the following areas:

1. Observation

The first period is primarily one of observation and will begin immediately upon arrival at the cooperating school. The length of the initial period will vary from several days to two weeks depending upon the individual situation and the length of the student teaching term. Observation is a continuing process and will recur at numerous times during the term. In many colleges, prospective teachers begin to observe music classes in public schools as early as their freshman year and continue to observe throughout their college years. You will find that ability to observe will develop along with awareness of the technical facets of teaching.

2. Planning and Teaching

Following the initial observation period you will enter into the planning and teaching phase of the student teaching program. You will learn to base your plans upon the points noted as you observe the cooperating teacher working with the class. With the assistance of your college supervisor and cooperating teacher, you will learn to select appropriate materials and methods of presentation according to the classes involved in the teaching assignment.

3. Evaluation

Evaluation, like observation, is a continual process. Ability to evaluate your teaching will grow through the use of tape recordings and films of your presentations and through suggestions offered by your cooperating teacher and college supervisor.

4. Compilation of Materials

During the student teaching period you will have numerous opportunities to study materials used in teaching instrumental, choral, and general music, theory and history. One of the primary activities of student teaching is the compilation and evaluation of these materials. The use and effectiveness of music, books, films, and records should be noted throughout your student teaching term.

Role of the Student Teacher

As a student teacher you are both a guest and an apprentice or assistant teacher in the cooperating school. You must operate within the framework set forth by the cooperating teacher since he is the person officially responsible for the musical growth of the members of the class or organization. Consequently, the role of the student teacher will vary according to the situation. Hopefully, you will have an opportunity to teach classes at various levels and to rehearse performing organizations. However, be aware of the fact that the primary concern of the cooperating teacher is for his students and their development. You will assist the cooperating teacher in a manner that best serves the members of the class or organization. This means that you may have limited experience in conducting the performing organizations. Your primary position in working with advanced instrumental or choral groups may be that of directing section rehearsals or working with individuals. At all times remember that it is your duty to serve where it will be of greatest benefit to the students. So long as you treat each student with respect, maintain a positive and enthusiastic attitude with high expectations for the students' accomplishments, and have a thorough knowledge of your subject and methods of presentation, you will make a significant contribution to the learning situation at your cooperating school.

Developing your position as a student teacher, however, is not an easy task. You are no longer a student in the classroom and have not yet assumed the position of a teacher. In addition to being an excellent musician and pedagogue, you will find your role in the cooperating school enhanced through the development of the following personal attributes:

1. Appearance

Appropriate dress for both men and women is very important. Choice of colors, length of dress, type of neckline, choice and amount of make-up, type of shirt, wearing a tie, hair style, heel height, and neatness are among the factors that are important in making a good appearance in the cooperating school. Good taste and considered choices in attire will give you an extra touch of maturity and should prove helpful as you establish your role as a teacher.

Sufficient rest is a necessity if you are to appear at your best. Tiredness, with its attendant lack of vitality and alertness, will affect your appearance and will cause you to be less effective as a student teacher. Achieving a rested condition poses a problem for many college students. For some, it involves a rearrangement of personal schedules; for some, it means a totally new approach to the management of time and energy. One important factor in preventing tiredness is a light college hour load. In many colleges the student teacher has no other courses during the student teaching term, thereby permitting him to give his entire attention to student teaching. You must work out a schedule whereby you can function most effectively in the student teaching setting.

2. *Poise and Emotional Stability*

The superior music teacher maintains control of his feelings, leaves his personal problems outside the classroom, has good rapport with his students and fellow faculty members, and is quick to show a sense of humor. The ability to remain calm in tense situations is an important asset in teaching. The pleasant quality of a well modulated voice can help you portray the poise necessary for working with young people. Ability to use your own speaking voice properly is very important. The resonant, clearly projected voice effected by adequate breath support will help to prevent fatigue and at the same time will keep the attention and interest of your pupils. Nonhesitant but slow well-articulated speech will gain the confidence of your pupils. Of course, avoid monotony by varying word emphasis and inflection. When a loss of emotional control is evidenced by a change in voice quality, the student teacher immediately finds himself in a disadvantageous position with his students. Although it may be necessary, upon occasion, to raise your voice to achieve a result, you should do so only when you think it will be effective and when you are in full control of your emotions. Equally important in the speech area is your consistent use of correct English. This includes the avoidance of excessive use of slang and casual expressions such as "o.k."

Exercising patience is conducive to poise and will help in working with your students. The student teacher who thinks he will be successful in every teaching attempt is unrealistic. The patience to try another method, to wait for the next opportunity to work out a problem, to work within the framework of the cooperating teacher's philosophy rather than his own, and to deal with each student in a controlled manner gives evidence of poise and maturity.

3. *Manners*

Good manners and courtesy are important to you personally and to the students with whom you are working. As a guest in the cooperating school you must display a consideration for others. For example, you will need to adjust smoking and coffee drinking habits to those of the persons with whom you work. Take your cue from your cooperating teacher and conform to the example set by him.

At the conclusion of the student teaching term you should show further evidence of good manners through the expression of gratitude for having been allowed the opportunity to work in the cooperating school. Letters of appreciation are due the cooperating teacher, the principal, and the college supervisor.

Role of the College Supervisor

The college supervisor is employed by the university for the purpose of assisting you in deriving the greatest possible value from the student teaching experience. The role of the college supervisor varies according to the organizational plan of the student teaching program at the university. For example, in the laboratory program, the college supervisor frequently has the dual role of teaching methods classes in the college and teaching preparatory school classes in a cooperating school. In this type of program the student teacher works with the college professor rather than a cooperating teacher.

Traditionally, the college supervisor is responsible for providing assistance as the student teacher works with a cooperating teacher in a cooperating school. In this role, the college supervisor is in close contact with the cooperating teacher throughout the student teaching period. It is the college supervisor's responsibility to acquaint the cooperating teacher with the student teaching expectations of the college. In turn, the college supervisor becomes acquainted with the cooperating teacher's approach to the student teaching experience. Conferences, both with and without the student teacher in attendance, are arranged as the situation dictates. Because of his objectivity, the college supervisor's perspective is helpful to both the cooperating teacher and the student teacher as they work together.

Regardless of the organizational plan—clinical or traditional—you will find that one of the most valuable experiences in your development as a music teacher occurs as the college supervisor observes you when you teach your students. Through the eyes of your college supervisor, you will be able to see yourself as your students see you. This gives you an opportunity to adjust mannerisms and approaches at frequent intervals. You will learn to evaluate your performance as a teacher and will begin to capitalize upon strong points and to improve weaknesses.

Another important role of the college supervisor is that of assisting in the acquisition and use of resource materials. The college supervisor who has taught elementary and secondary school music has a knowledge of proven techniques, an accumulation of materials, and many creative ideas. Seek his assistance as you plan for and teach the students at your assignment.

Role of the Cooperating Teacher

The cooperating teacher has a fundamental role in the student teaching program because of his close relationship to you and his students. His effectiveness will be the result of several factors:

1. His superiority in teaching music.
2. His belief in the value of the student teaching program.
3. His satisfaction in having a vital part in the training of a good teacher.
4. His willingness to share new ideas with the student teacher.

The cooperating teacher will be of primary importance in introducing you to the students, the faculty and staff members, and the total school program. In the initial conferences he will explain some of the following points:

1. His basic teaching philosophy.
2. His immediate and long-range goals and plans for you as a student teacher.
3. The daily class schedule, including a description of the grouping of the students.
4. A schedule of meetings including faculty, PTA, parent organizations, and school-community meetings which you must attend as a student teacher.
5. Clarification of the working relationship.
6. Discussion of evaluation and its application to the student teaching experience.

A portion of your orientation into the program at the cooperating school will come through the first observation period. Your cooperating teacher will use this time for the purpose of providing a gradual transition into planning and teaching. For example, you will probably begin your tenure as a student teacher by assisting the cooperating teacher in some of the following:

1. Keeping attendance records.
2. Helping with the care and distribution of teaching materials.
3. Helping with the physical arrangements of the room: chairs, music stands, ventilation, lighting.
4. Typing and mimeographing materials.
5. Assisting various students by moving about the room during the class or rehearsal.
6. Studying the instructional material used by the cooperating teacher; filing for future use titles of music, books, and other materials.

7. Participating, through discussion with the cooperating teacher, in planning.

As the cooperating teacher observes your management of the daily routine, he will evaluate your skill in working with students and your readiness for planning and teaching. Toward the end of the initial observation period, you and your cooperating teacher will discuss your first teaching assignment. He may ask you to submit lesson plans in advance so that he can check them, discuss them with you, and allow you sufficient time to make necessary changes.

The cooperating teacher will encourage use of ideas which you have developed during your college training. However, he will be aware of the fact that assistance may be needed in applying your ideas to the appropriate situation. Up to the point of student teaching it is possible that you have only seen others apply effective teaching techniques. You may not be fully aware of the fact that the technique must be selected to fit the situation. For example, a teaching procedure may be very effective with one fifth grade music class but totally inappropriate for another fifth grade class within the same school. The cooperating teacher will assist in the selection of methods and materials suitable for the specific class involved.

Note that a master teacher develops, in part, as a result of his knowledge of the subject and his skill in methods of presentation. He has had the benefit of years of experience. He capitalizes upon not only his own ideas, but also those of his colleagues. He is a creative teacher in that he is able to use ideas in a unique way. Consequently, do not hesitate to adapt procedures used by your cooperating teacher and your college professors. The cooperating teacher will assist you in knowing how to use borrowed procedures as a basis for building a unique approach.

The Cooperating School

One of the goals of the student teaching program is to gain insight into the total school program. The principal of the cooperating school will explain, in varying degrees of detail, many facets of the school program. These generally include:

1. The scope of the school curriculum and the place of music in the curriculum.

2. General school policies such as discipline, faculty meeting attendance, and special duties.

3. Clarification of routine procedures, such as reporting to the school and notification procedures in case of illness.

4. Discussion of the role of the school in the community, and the importance of attendance at PTA and other school-community activities.

5. Explanation of the roles of faculty and staff members.

6. Introduction to the physical plant and materials available.

The principal may have several conferences with you and he may observe your work from time to time. He most certainly will check with your cooperating teacher concerning your progress. The recommendation of the principal may be of assistance in helping you to obtain a teaching position in the future.

As a student teacher, become acquainted with other members of the faculty and staff as you attempt to formulate concepts concerning the operation of the school as a whole. Staff members—all persons working in a capacity other than teaching—provide an important service to student and faculty. You should become acquainted with counselors, librarians, nurses, custodians, and secretaries. An understanding of the roles of staff members is an important part of your education. A respect for the importance of staff positions in the total school life will help you to establish a habit of forming pleasant, effective relationships with your co-workers.

Suggestions for Further Reading

Andrews, Frances M., *"Guideposts for Beginning Teachers,"* Music Educators Journal, *LIV, No. 2 (1967), 37-38.*

Benson, Earl C., *"Modular Scheduling in Music,"* Music Educators Journal, *LIV, No. 4 (1967), 55-56.*

Dunlop, Richard S., *"Toward Improved Professional Practice Under Flexible Modular Scheduling,"* Journal of Teacher Education, *XIX, No. 2 (1968),* 159.

Gaines, Joan, *"Secondary Principals Comment on Music,"* Music Educators Journal, *LIV, No. 8 (1968), 85-86.*

Kuhn, Wolfgang, *"Microteaching,"* Music Educators Journal, *LV, No. 4 (1968), 49-53.*

Leeder, Joseph A., and William S. Haynie, Music Education in the High School. Englewood Cliffs, N.J.: Prentice-Hall, Inc., 1964, Chapter 9.

McQuerrey, Lawrence H., *"Microrehearsal,"* Music Educators Journal, *LV, No. 4 (1968), 48-53.*

Roberts, Charles, *"Flexible Modular Scheduling and Instrumental Music,"* The Instrumentalist, *XXIV, No. 1 (1968), 77-78.*

Verrastro, Ralph E., *"Improving Student-Teacher Supervision,"* Music Educators Journal, *LIV, No. 3 (1967), 81-83.*

2

Observation

By the time you enter the student teaching program you should have had numerous opportunities, during your early college years, to observe music classes and rehearsals at various grade levels. If this has been the case, you will have developed an awareness of the effect of class routine and teaching techniques upon the advancement of the musical organization. You will have viewed classroom rehearsal control and will have developed theories concerning methods of working with students. You will have seen various teachers as they employ contrasting methods with similar results. You will have gained a respect for teaching and will have come to recognize teaching as an art.

Observation is one of the most important facets in your development as a teacher. Learning to observe is a gradual process that requires careful guidance. For this reason, a guide to the observation of music classes is presented in the following pages to help you to observe class routine, class control, and teaching techniques. You should also have an opportunity to observe teachers and classes in various curriculum areas. Valuable insights may be gained by watching master teachers in non-music classes. You will also have an opportunity to grow in the understanding of your pupils and their attitudes and interests as you visit other classes. Still another advantage of this observation is that you become acquainted with the total curriculum. Most of the items in the guide will apply to instrumental, choral, and general music classes at each of the three levels—beginning, intermediate, and advanced.

Class Routine

The format by which the class is conducted will have a significant effect upon the musical growth of the organization. Since time is a precious commodity and must be spent wisely if the sessions are to be of value, the cooperating teacher will have devised procedures which facilitate daily routine matters connected with the class. Your initial task, as a student teacher, is to study class routine through daily observation in order to be better prepared to make the most of the time allotted you when you begin teaching.

In observing class routine, the following items should be considered:

1. Room Set-Up

The condition of the room when the students enter is a major factor in class control, since this can have a part in setting a mood for the rehearsal. When possible, chairs and stands should be in place for the rehearsal prior to the entrance of the students.

In instrumental music, the following plans are frequently used by directors in handling the room setup for the class or the instrumental rehearsal:

Plan One: The director sets up the room. This is one of the less satisfactory plans since the director is frequently busy between rehearsals. Students, administrative duties, or consultations with visitors may require his attention.

Plan Two: The students from the previous class set up for the next group. While this plan is workable, it is difficult to enforce because the students may see little purpose in setting up for another class. Also, this plan usually calls for constant supervision from the director in order to see that the job is done.

Plan Three: The director appoints a set-up crew from the musical organization or class. The crew members set up the room while the other students are getting their music folios and instruments. Sometimes one person from each section is appointed to the crew. In this case, the crew member's stand partner is responsible for getting the music and both instruments.

In many choral rehearsal rooms permanent risers are standard equipment, especially at the secondary level. In the absence of permanent risers, portable standing risers along with chairs are frequently included in the room so that the director may conduct some of the rehearsals in performance position.

Since the elementary school choir is often too large for the ordinary elementary classroom, rehearsals are frequently held in the school cafeteria or auditorium. If portable chairs are used, the set-up should be arranged prior to the rehearsal so that the children may be quickly seated in an orderly fashion.

The room set-up for the general music classes varies according to the level of instruction. In the elementary school the following arrangements are among those used:

Plan One: The music teacher remains in his classroom and the children come to that room for their lesson. In this case, the music, materials, books, and instruments are at hand for both pupils and teacher.

Plan Two: The music teacher goes to the children, travelling from room to room. He uses a cart to carry music books, instruments, and a record player as he moves about the school. Sometimes a piano is moved from room to room by student assistants.

The general music classes in the secondary school are usually held in the choral music room thereby making readily available the materials needed for the classes.

As a student teacher, consider the set-up plan used by your cooperating teacher. Guide questions for this area should include:

1. Are chairs and stands in place when the students enter the room? If so, who is responsible for the room set-up?
2. Is the piano appropriately placed for rehearsals?
3. Are the tape recorder and phonograph readily available for use as needed?
4. Are chairs provided for visitors?
5. Are the lighting and room temperature adjusted?

Evaluate the effectiveness of the room set-up at your cooperating school. Alternate plans should be noted when applicable.

2. Storage Facilities

The method of storing music, instruments, recordings, and uniforms should be noted as you view the physical arrangement of the classroom or rehearsal hall. Rehearsal time can be saved if music folios and instruments are clearly labeled and kept in a specific location so that the students can locate their equipment and take their seats with a minimum of confusion. At the beginning of the class period note the time taken as the students prepare to play or sing. In cases of abnormal delay, study the problem and work out tentative solutions.

3. Music Distribution

When possible, music should be placed in the folios and books should be distributed prior to the rehearsal or class. However, if the music librarian is a student, it is possible that he will need to distribute parts and take up music during the class period. In the elementary school the children are frequently involved with the distribution of music and materials, thus giving each child an opportunity to share responsibilities.

In instrumental rehearsals section leaders can assist the student librarian in the handling of music so that music for the entire section can be issued and recalled from the first stands. This makes the members of the section responsible to the section leader. All parts should be numbered and issued to the music folio bearing the same number. For example, copy number two of the first violin part would be placed in music folio number two of the first violin section. The students playing at the second stand are then responsible for all music labeled first violin, stand two.

The important consideration in the distribution of music is the existence of some type of organized plan. Study the method used by your cooperating teacher and evaluate its effectiveness with regard to consumption of class time.

4. Students' Entrance

As the students enter the room focus your attention upon them. Much can be learned about students by watching them as they prepare to go to work. Think about the following questions with regard to the students' entrance into the room:

1. Do the students quickly locate their music and instruments and assume their assigned places?
2. Are certain students consistently slow in taking their places? If so, what are the reasons for their delay?
3. What is the reaction of the cooperating teacher to the slower students?
4. What does the teacher do while the students enter the room?

Observe the cooperating teacher's presence and obvious eagerness in beginning the rehearsal promptly as generally reflected by the students' interest in the class. Observe the cooperating teacher's utilization of this brief entrance time as he shows personal concern for individuals by listening momentarily to a student's problem or by offering words of greeting.

5. Chair Assignments

a. Instrumental Classes and Organizations—Unless there is a specific reason for daily rotation of chairs, it is a good plan to have each student in the orchestra or band assigned to a specific chair within the section. In this way a student may become accustomed to a stand partner and music can be accounted for with greater ease. Chair assignment methods vary in degree from highly competitive challenge systems to the assignment of chairs by the director. Study the method used by your cooperating teacher and evaluate the effectiveness of this plan.

In seating the orchestra or band by sections, your cooperating teacher will generally consider the following points:

1. The similarity of parts: for example, the instruments that are primarily

responsible for rhythmic effects would be grouped in one area of the set-up. This might place percussion, tuba, horns, and string bass together. The music has a part in determining the seating plan.

2. The ability of the sections: frequently, strong sections are seated in such a way that they will reinforce weaker sections. To illustrate, the placement of the piano at the back of the string orchestra will often help younger musicians in both intonation and rhythm. When there is a balance problem, smaller sections are sometimes seated closer to the audience.

3. The acoustics of the room: through experimentation, the director finds the best seating in the specific rehearsal hall or auditorium. If the sections within the orchestra or band are to balance, acoustics must be considered in planning the seating. For example, the French horns would rarely be placed directly in front of a smooth wall because the sound would be magnified and reflected off the wall and toward the audience.

Discuss the seating plan with your cooperating teacher. If time permits, it is possible that he will let you experiment with the seating arrangement of your class or organization.

b. Choirs—Since choir seating, unlike that of the orchestra and band, rarely involves competition, the selection of the seating arrangement is usually the director's responsibility. In many instances the seating is arranged so that the weak section is placed in the center front of the choir. Or, if one section is numerically larger, it may be spread across the back or the outer edges of the choir. Many choral directors use sectionalized seating for the rehearsal and change, especially in the advanced choir, to a quartet or part against part arrangement for performance. Because the elementary school choir rehearsal time is usually limited, it is especially important that a seating arrangement be established quickly. Children react and learn well in a stable situation.

Whatever the seating plan, choral directors generally consider the individual voices as they seek to effect a blended, unified choral sound. The seating arrangement for the choral organization may change from time to time within the school year depending upon changing voices, new personnel, and the difficulty and vocal arrangement of the compositions to be performed.

c. General Music Classes—In the elementary school, if the classroom size permits, a space should be left open for singing games and rhythmic activities. Seating is adjusted as children form groups for part singing.

In the junior and senior high school general music class, the seating plan generally follows a sectionalized vocal part arrangement. Sectionalized seating may consist only of separating boys and girls, since part singing in the general music class is less demanding than in the advanced choir. The seating arrangement may change during the term as the pupils gain proficiency in singing and in reading music.

6. *Attendance Check*

The daily attendance check must not interfere with the class time allotted to the students. Note the method used in reporting daily attendance at your assignment. It is possible that the cooperating teacher will delegate this responsibility to a student assistant so that he may be free to attend to the needs of individual students. In the case of large organizations, such as bands, the section leaders may be assigned the responsibility of taking attendance for their sections and reporting daily to the student secretary. The secretary then fills out the attendance report and clears it with the music teacher.

7. *Class Dismissal*

The students should be dismissed at the end of the class by the music teacher rather than the school bell. At the close of the class period the individual student must accept the responsibility for the storage of his music, books, and instrument. Note the condition of the room after the students have left. You will need to learn, from your cooperating teacher, what happens when a student leaves his music out or fails to accept other responsibilities.

To conclude, the music teacher is responsible for the establishment and enforcement of the class or rehearsal plan. A clearly defined routine is an essential factor in the development of the music class regardless of the level of the students.

Class Control

Teachers and student teachers frequently state that a lack of control over the class is their number one problem in teaching. Unless a teacher has the attention of his students, his efforts will be wasted. Some of the points you will need to consider in studying class control are as follows:

1. *Class Routine*

The class should be planned so that the majority of the students' time is spent working with music. Items such as room set-up, music distribution, attendance check, and lesson routine must be considered as factors affecting the control of the class or rehearsal. Students appreciate the teacher who has the routine planned so that a maximum of time is spent in musical endeavors.

2. *Understanding of Students*

The teacher must have a sincere interest in helping his students—both in musical and non-musical problems. Respect must be shown for each member of the class regardless of his musical ability or intelligence level. The music teacher should be as interested in his intermediate instrumental class and his training choir as he is in his advanced performing organization.

Your cooperating teacher will not work with each of his students in the same way. He will consider individual differences—mental, physical, and emotional—before determining an appropriate course of action. For example, one student may thrive on praise while another works best when praise is used sparingly.

You can learn much by watching your cooperating teacher as he works through human relations problems areas with his students. Consider the following questions as you seek an understanding of teacher-pupil rapport and its development:

1. Does the cooperating teacher respect each student and offer his assistance to individuals without showing favoritism?

2. Does the cooperating teacher always consider the student's point of view before making a decision that will affect him?

3. Does the cooperating teacher refrain from embarrassing the student in front of his peers?

4. Do the students leave the class or rehearsal with a positive feeling about themselves?

3. *Understanding of Music and Teaching*

A teacher must have the knowledge necessary to help his students in their musical growth and he must have the ability to project this knowledge. It will be advantageous to develop several approaches to the same musical problem. When you teach, you will then be in a position to select an approach most suitable to the specific situation. You will also need to formulate an understanding of sequence in presentation of material. By observing a skilled teacher you will note that he makes allowances for individual differences by providing materials of varying difficulty according to the needs of his students.

Since class control is greatly affected by the timing of the presentation, observe that your cooperating teacher paces the class presentation according to the needs and interest span of his students. Before the material being presented grows stale, he will switch to contrasting materials. The teacher is constantly striving to find a way whereby he can challenge his students without discouraging them.

4. Rehearsal Discipline

It is extremely important for the teacher to maintain control over his actions in tense moments. He cannot argue with a student in front of the class and expect to maintain the respect of his students. As a student teacher, you will have to deal with teacher-pupil problems because all teachers face discipline problems from time to time. Learn to deal effectively with different types of problems by watching the results of the action taken by other teachers and by trying out various techniques.

Unfortunately, the teacher is frequently a contributor to the problems that occur in the classroom. Some of the mistakes made by teachers and student teachers are as follows:

1. Coming to the rehearsal unprepared.
2. Failing to begin the rehearsal promptly.
3. Wasting time trying to locate music and materials.
4. Caring for all class routines personally rather than delegating some of them to students.
5. Failing to adjust lighting, temperature, and seating.
6. Engaging in emotionalized behavior or throwing a temper tantrum.
7. Interrupting a rehearsal to argue with a student.
8. Talking excessively to the students during the rehearsal.
9. Utilizing inappropriate incentives for learning.
10. Giving vague rehearsal instructions.
11. Oversimplifying explanations or stating them in terms beyond the students' ability to comprehend.
12. Working for excessive periods of time with one section of the ensemble or with one composition.
13. Failing to provide for ability differences among the students.,
14. Assigning work for home practice without proper explanation.
15. Allowing the students to leave the rehearsal hall when the bell rings without being dismissed.

The teacher should consistently guide his students toward the acceptance of responsibility and the development of self-discipline. Students need to learn to work independently if they are to progress in the music field. Study those students displaying high degrees of self-direction in an attempt to understand ways in which this characteristic may be fostered in the music class.

Teaching Techniques

For successful observation of your cooperating teacher as he teaches his classes you will need to develop an awareness of the facets involved in preparing for the class or the rehearsal and in presenting the materials. This means that you will need to consider the objectives of the class session, the selection, organization and presentation of materials, and the evaluation of teaching techniques. Special attention should be directed toward the following points:

1. The objectives of the class: long range and daily.
2. The manner in which the teacher introduces the day's activities.
3. The way in which maximum use of available time is made.
4. The sequential development of the lesson or rehearsal.
5. The variations in the teacher's methods of presentation as necessitated by the individual differences of his students.
6. The adaptation of the day's plan as made necessary by extraneous circumstances: change in school schedule due to assembly, homeroom, and other unpredictable events.
7. The pacing of the period: moving smoothly through various activities, and avoiding boredom and inattention through sensitivity to the students and the situation.
8. The closing of the period: the music or activity selected to end the period so that a positive effect will stay with the students.

Each of the above points will be discussed in the following chapters as they pertain to instrumental, choral, general music, theory, and history classes.

Suggestions for Further Reading

Berg, Herman, "Conductors Corner—Use of the Face, Body, and Left Hand," The Instrumentalist, *XXII, No. 9 (1968), 74-76, 77.*

Dearborn, Norman, "String Tuning and Pegs," The Instrumentalist, *XXIII, No. 1 (1968), 81-85.*

Douglass, C. William, "Arturo Toscanini, The Maestro of Us All," Music Educators Journal, *LIV, No. 6 (1968), 69-71.*

Goldman, Richard Franko, The Wind Band: Its Literature and Technique. *Boston; Allyn & Bacon, Inc., 1961, Chapter 9.*

Hoffer, Charles R., "Teaching Useful Knowledge in Rehearsal," Music Educators Journal, *LII, No. 5 (1966), 49-51, 90-94.*

House, Robert W., Instrumental Music in Today's Schools. *Englewood Cliffs, N.J.: Prentice-Hall, Inc., 1964, Chapters 2 and 3.*

Kuhn, Wolfgang, Instrumental Music, *Boston: Allyn & Bacon, Inc., 1962, Chapter 3.*

Matchett, Robert, "Warm up Correctly for a Better Band," The Instrumentalist, *XXIII, No. 1 (1968), 70-72.*

Purrington, Bruce R., "Team Teaching in the Musical Arts," Music Educators Journal, *LIII, No. 8 (1967), 135-137.*

Sur, William Raymond, and Charles Francis Schuller, Music Education for Teen-Agers. *New York: Harper & Row, Publishers, 1958, Chapters 2, 3, 5, and 12.*

3

Planning and Teaching: Instrumental Music

The essence of the student teaching experience in instrumental music will become apparent as you organize your materials and present them to your students. When planning for and teaching classes, you will need to consider the following areas:

1. Performance problems: identification and solution
2. Lesson planning
3. Presentation
4. Evaluation
5. Compilation of materials

Performance Problems: Identification—Solution

During the periods of observation you will have begun to recognize some of the needs of the members of the organization. As the students play a composition they will show areas of weakness. The primary phase of the teacher's work is to learn to identify the source of the musical problem and to provide methods whereby the problem may be overcome.

An important factor in identifying causes of performance problems is the teacher's sensitivity to students. A teacher can see almost as many problems in a rehearsal as he can hear. For example, the flutes are having difficulty in the execution of a rapid passage and the teacher notes that one student is raising his fingers too high in going from note to note, while another is taking a breath at the wrong place in the phrase. To obtain clues from the students concerning individual and group performance problems, you must be highly sensitive to each musician during the rehearsal. If a student could relate the reason for his problem in a specific passage, he would have little need for a teacher.

One of the basic principles of teaching is that the teacher must be aware of all possible causes of a performance problem before he can intelligently select a method that will lead to a solution to the problem. Consequently, develop "sets of solutions" to performance problems prior to the rehearsal. The larger the repertoire of solutions, the greater are the possibilities of dealing with the problem successfully. To illustrate, suppose that a teacher, in rehearsing an organization, finds a serious intonation problem in a specific passage. He recalls that his college band director used *Bach Chorales* to teach his students to play in tune. Therefore, he decides to use these as tune-up materials. However, there are a number of instances, such as the following, in which the use of chorales will not solve an intonation problem:

1. *Failure of the Instrument:* Is a particular clarinet consistently flat? If so perhaps a new barrel is needed. Is a key on an out of tune saxophone bent? Do the pegs on the fifth chair cello slip?
2. *Inability to Produce the Pitch*: Is the violin student unable to play in tune because of an incorrect left hand position? Is a poorly formed embouchure the basis of the trumpeter's problem in intonation?
3. *Failure to Listen*: Is the problem one of failure to listen, or is there a lack of awareness of the correct sound of the passage? Is a physical problem involved?
4. *Rhythm:* Is rhythm, rather than intonation, causing the organization's problem? Do the students understand where the conductor's beat lies? If not, are some students playing slightly ahead while others play after the beat? If this happens throughout the organization, the distortion may lead the director to assume that there is a severe intonation problem when, in reality, the problem is rhythmic.

When you learn to identify accurately the cause of the problem before prescribing the solution, your growth in teaching should be significant and your confidence in working with the instrumental music organization should develop immeasurably.

Some of the problem areas common to school orchestra and band classes are: intonation, rhythm, dynamics, balance, style, tone production, articulation, and phrasing. It is possible to develop sets of solutions for the problems that occur in each of the performance areas. Learn to anticipate the occurrence of specific performance problems and to be ready to provide solutions for them. When teaching is viewed from this perspective, it is definitely a field for the highly creative person.

Lesson Planning

As you prepare to begin the teaching phase, your task is that of planning, with the assistance of your cooperating teacher and college supervisor, for the first class or rehearsal.

The question of the need for lesson plans often arises during the student teaching period. You may see your cooperating teacher conduct an apparently effortless lesson without the use of any type of written guide. When this happens, it is highly probable that he has studied the score so thoroughly and knows his students so well that he only appears to react spontaneously when he directs the group. This situation is much the same as that which occurs when a fine concert pianist makes a complicated concerto appear to be simple. However, we know that the performing artist has spent endless hours preparing for the concert. Be assured that the artist teacher seriously considers each lesson prior to his performance as a teacher.

In planning for teaching, it is necessary to keep in mind the fact that the keynote of good teaching is flexibility. It is possible to have a beautifully designed lesson fall flat simply because of a lack of awareness on the part of the teacher. One example of the need to adjust occurs on the day when a special event precedes the instrumental class. It is unrealistic to expect students to be enthusiastic over the study of a three octave scale if they have just come to class from a football pep rally. You will, in a case such as this, need to adjust your lesson plan so that it better coincides with the tempo of the events of the day.

Each instrumental music lesson or rehearsal should be an extension of the previous session. Consequently, it is necessary to consider the materials that need to be reviewed as well as the materials that are to be introduced. The purpose of the lesson will be determined by the needs of the students and the goals of the organization. This means that the formulation of the lesson plan will depend upon the analysis of the performance level of the students and the probable areas of difficulty within the music chosen for presentation. Again, the need for flexibility cannot be overstressed. For example, a teacher may plan to work with his string class by reviewing a bowing pattern before attempting to play a composition containing this pattern. He anticipates spending approximately five minutes on the bowing. When he begins to work with the students, he finds that their concept of bow distribution and style is such that additional time must be spent on the bowings. Also, the students seem to be highly receptive, on this particular day, to technical work. A situation such as this will call for a departure from the previous plan in order to capitalize upon the momentary needs and interest of the students in the class.

Although it is sometimes necessary to discard the lesson plan, it is still important to formulate a teaching outline prior to working with the class or organization. The following reasons point to the need for planning:

1. The fact that you take time to make an outline of a plan before going to the class means that you are forcing yourself to be more aware of the needs of your students.

2. If you are analyzing well, it is probable that the lesson plan will be workable more times than not.

3. It is much easier for you, as a beginning teacher, to depart from a plan than to give an impromptu teaching performance in front of your students.

The form of the lesson plan in instrumental music will vary according to your needs as a beginning teacher, the time allotted for the lesson, the type of materials to be covered, and the type of class for which the lesson is planned. The following forms should be among those considered in planning for the instrumental music class or rehearsal:

Form A: You will witness the result of one type of lesson plan when you see your cooperating teacher list, on the chalkboard, the order of music for the daily rehearsal. This is the shortest form of a plan and is used frequently by experienced orchestra and band directors. This procedure is helpful in two ways. First, the students in the organization can get their music in order prior to the rehearsal. Second, it provides an outline for the director to use in conducting the rehearsal. In arriving at this plan, your cooperating teacher will have considered the following points:

1. Performance commitments of the organization

2. Consideration of the needs of the students as evidenced by the previous rehearsal

3. Technical materials which may be advantageously used according to the music to be rehearsed

4. Variety of musical experience, including recordings, films, and clinicians

5. Time allotted for the rehearsal

Form B: You will, in all probability, need to outline the steps you will use in teaching a specific technique or in introducing a new piece of music. This type of detailed planning is generally appropriate when you are responsible for teaching a technique, such as vibrato, for the first time or when you are responsible for a portion of the lesson.

Figure 3-1 is an example of step-wise planning. A teacher found that three members of his clarinet section were having rhythmic problems in a passage. He discovered that the students lacked the ability necessary to count the passage aloud. The students had always waited until they heard their director play the passage and then they would imitate what they heard. Sight reading was impossible for them. The teacher planned steps illustrated in Figure 3-1 and used them in sequence in teaching these students to count.

The teacher planned to spend one class period introducing his five step plan. Each day thereafter, he planned to spend a limited amount of time

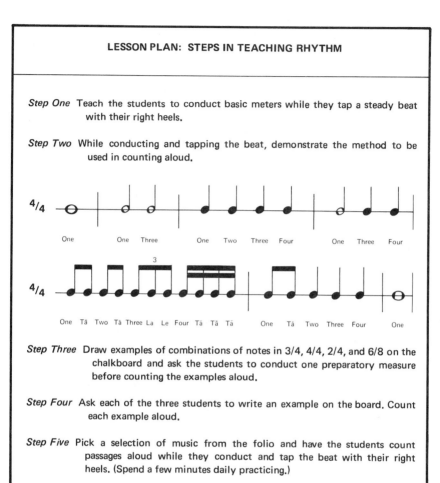

LESSON PLAN: STEPS IN TEACHING RHYTHM

Step One Teach the students to conduct basic meters while they tap a steady beat with their right heels.

Step Two While conducting and tapping the beat, demonstrate the method to be used in counting aloud.

Step Three Draw examples of combinations of notes in 3/4, 4/4, 2/4, and 6/8 on the chalkboard and ask the students to conduct one preparatory measure before counting the examples aloud.

Step Four Ask each of the three students to write an example on the board. Count each example aloud.

Step Five Pick a selection of music from the folio and have the students count passages aloud while they conduct and tap the beat with their right heels. (Spend a few minutes daily practicing.)

Figure 3-1.

hearing the students count aloud before having them play specific passages from their music. This type of planning can have a significant effect upon the clarity of the presentation.

Form C: During student teaching, you will probably use a topical plan in organizing the instrumental music class or rehearsal. In Figure 3-2, the major topics or sections are tuning, warm-up, review, new materials, and concluding materials. Specific objectives and procedures are listed under each heading. A space is left at the side of the plan for the purpose of evaluating each portion of the lesson. The evaluation section can be used to make memos concerning the needs for the next lesson.

LESSON PLAN: INTERMEDIATE STRING CLASS

Procedure	Evaluation

I. Tuning:
  A. Review tuning by double stops
  B. Check individual tuning
 	
II. Warm-up:
  A. Bow exercises
  B. Tone production exercises
 	
III. Review:
  A. Vibrato exercises
  B. *Symphony for Young People,* Williams
    1. Play movement I
    2. Check: Harmonics
         Bow recovery
 	
IV. Introduce:
  A. Baroque Style—Concerto Grosso
    1. Discuss the style
    2. Play record to illustrate
    3. Review style
  B. Introduce—Concerto Grosso, Farish
    1. Play movement I (Orch. plays)
    2. Review style discussion
    3. Play portions of record
    4. Play section A of composition
    5. Review style again, if needed
 	
V. Conclusion:
  A. Play folk songs by rote
  B. Play original melodies	

Figure 3-2.

You will, in all probability, find it advantageous to use a combination of the three basic lesson plan forms. Plans B and C should be used frequently in the beginning stages of your development as an instrumental music teacher. Plan A may be used along with plans B and C and may eventually replace these as you become skilled in pedagogy.

The type of music experiences planned for the group should differ little in moving from organizing for the beginning class to planning for the senior high school rehearsal. Each group should have the opportunity to develop performance techniques and knowledge of music as a result of the activities of the class or the rehearsal. The instrumental music class is designed primarily for the furtherance of technique and is generally associated with the beginning stages of development. The rehearsal is used for the preparation of music for public presentations and is the primary activity of the advanced organization. However, there is an over-lapping. The beginning class should participate in at least one public performance during the year, and the advanced organization should have numerous opportunities for technical and musical development along with the performances. The type of class for which you are responsible in planning and teaching depends upon your level of certification. The objectives of the elementary and secondary instrumental classes are generally as follows:

1. Elementary School Classes

If you work in the elementary school, you are primarily responsible for helping the students in these areas:

1. The formulation of good basic positions.
2. The development of a concept of the sound of the instrument and the group.
3. The development of the ability to produce a good sound on the instrument.
4. The development of a sensitivity for musical expression through the awareness and execution of dynamics, phrasing, and articulation.

Since the demands for the ability to read music are usually less urgent for elementary school beginners than for junior high school beginners, more time can probably be spent with rote approaches in the lower grades. Also, younger students are highly responsive to repetition since the entire scope of the learning process is fresh to them. It is important to keep in mind that learning is a gradual process. Patience is needed in working with the elementary school child. Language patterns must be adapted to the level of the child without talking down to him. A constant watch must be maintained in order to know when the child begins to tire of an exercise or a piece of music so that something else can be introduced. If you plan to use a method book with the elementary class, review the following ways in which it may be effectively used:

1. The exercises in the method book are tools to be used in dealing with specific problems. The teacher must be able to recognize the problem and to select the exercise suitable for use in working with the situation. The method book is simply a time saving device for the teacher because of the inclusion of several exercises in a single book. The method book should never become the teacher of the class. The teacher must be selective in the assignment of exercises from a method book. It would not be intelligent to begin the year with exercise number one and to play all of the exercises in the book in the order in which they are written.

2. The method book does not begin with the easiest exercise and end with the most difficult. This is impossible because the difficulty concept changes as the teacher moves from student to student. Where one student will find exercise number one difficult, another will play it with ease. Again, choose material selectively.

3. The method book must appeal to the students in the class if progress is to be made. Since it is possible to have beginning classes in both elementary and secondary schools, the teacher must consider the age of the student when he selects a method book. It is not reasonable to think that a high school beginner will accept a method book if it is designed for elementary school students and is composed of songs that have nursery rhyme titles.

4. The method book should not be accepted as an authoritative approach to the instrument unless the teacher has verified its contents.

2. *Secondary School Classes*

As a student teacher in the secondary school, you will work with beginning, intermediate, and performing groups. Teaching the beginning and intermediate classes at the secondary level should be very much like teaching elementary school instrumental classes. With the secondary student the vocabulary can be larger and you can probably move somewhat faster than is possible in the elementary school, but you will still be teaching basic techniques of performance. As a student teacher, you will probably have numerous opportunities to teach the beginning and intermediate classes in the secondary school. However, with the advanced performing organization, you may be cast in a completely different role. The performance commitments of the orchestra or band may be such that your cooperating teacher cannot give you a block of teaching time with the organization. Consequently, you will probably conduct section rehearsals and special ensembles more often than you will actually conduct the complete organization.

In some cases, band student teachers at the secondary level are given the opportunity to plan and teach a football halftime show. While the student teacher is basically on his own in this type of experience, he should still consult frequently with his cooperating teacher and college supervisor as he plans and teaches the music and formations.

Presentation

Presentation is a crucial phase of teaching at each level. Consider the following points as you study techniques of presentation in instrumental music:

1. Involving the Class While Working with an Individual or a Section

In all probability, as a beginning student teacher, you have had more experience in teaching one student at a time than you have in teaching a group. Learn techniques of involving all of the members of the organization as you work with a section or an individual. You may find it advantageous to draw students into the discussion by asking them to offer suggestions for improvement of performance problems encountered by both themselves and their peers.

2. Seeing Individuals Within the Group

Develop the ability to see individual students as you look at the group. Also, be able to retain the impression received. For example, you will not usually want to stop in the middle of the class to correct a bowing problem unless this pertains to each member of the section. Consequently, you will need to recall the error so that you can return to the problem after the musical example has been concluded. Through this ability, individual corrections may be made during the rehearsal.

3. Correcting Performance Problems Immediately

Problems do not generally disappear with time unless the teacher offers consistent suggestions for improvement. Frequently, individual performance problems, such as posture, intonation, and rhythm will be ignored due to an erroneous assumption that the problem will leave as the student becomes more experienced. The skilled instrumental teacher realizes that problems should be attacked as soon as they are recognized. If the problem is unique to one student, arrangements should be made to assist the student on an individual basis. For the most part students will have similar performance problems, especially during the early stages of their development.

4. Speaking Distinctly

Speech patterns often present problems in the student teacher's presentation. Typical problem areas are: speaking too rapidly, speaking too softly, and speaking with a lack of variety in inflection.

Make frequent use of a tape recorder for the purpose of checking your vocal presentation. It is sometimes effective and revealing to start the tape recorder at the beginning of the class period and let it record the entire session. When possible video tapes of your presentation should be made so that you can study these following the rehearsal.

5. Giving Students Enough Time to Prepare to Play

The students in the class or musical organization must learn to prepare to play when the director raises the baton. Frequently, the student teacher will make the mistake of giving the downbeat before the students have adequate time to get their instruments in playing position. You will need to work with your students so that they can know what is expected when you raise the baton. This act will need to be practiced in the same manner as other exercises.

6. Adjusting Chairs and Stands

Students usually need assistance in adjusting their stands to the proper height and position so that they can see both the music and the director. Although you may notice an improvement in performance when your students stand or when they play without music, teach them the proper position for playing when seated. They must learn to adjust their stands to a proper height and position. It is frequently necessary to ask students to make adjustments according to your position on the podium.

7. Analyzing Performance Problems

The beginning student teacher frequently recognizes the existence of a performance problem but fails to recommend a proper procedure in dealing with the problem. For example, he may recognize a rhythmic problem but he may not discover the reason for the problem, since the following items may affect the performance:

1. inability to recognize the conductor's beat
2. inability to count the passage
3. physical problems, such as lifting the fingers too high or inappropriate bow distribution.

Before prescribing a possible solution, you must know the specific reason for the performance problem.

8. Providing a Good Example Through Performance

Too often a trial and error system is used in teaching instrumental music classes. For example, the teacher tells the student that he does not like the tone produced but fails to provide an example of the preferred sound. Consequently, the student has nothing to use for comparison. You must provide musical examples through your own performance on an instrument or through the use of appropriate recordings.

9. Presenting Steps in a Logical Order in Teaching a Skill

It is essential that materials be presented in a logical sequence of steps. Too often, a student sees only the finished product of a performance skill, such as vibrato or double tonguing. He tries to imitate this and finds that it is much too difficult for him to accomplish. In reality, what the student has done is to attempt the impossible by starting with the last step rather than the first. The secret of teaching lies in the development of the ability to present, in sequence, all steps necessary for the performance. You will find that the mastery of a performance task becomes difficult for your student when he fails to understand the logical order of the steps involved in the skill.

Evaluation

As an instrumental student teacher, you will need to consider the following areas in studying evaluation:

1. evaluating individual performances of students
2. evaluating the performing organization
3. evaluating planning and teaching

Evaluating Individual Students

Study plans used in grading individual students in the instrumental class or organization. Among those plans used are the following:

1. Competition with Other Students

The challenge system is among those used by directors in evaluating students. In this plan, students are given an opportunity to advance in chair placement by "challenging" those persons who are sitting in a higher chair. The use of a challenge system is optional with the director. Consequently, you may or may not find this used by your cooperating teacher.

2. Individual Improvement

The musical growth of the student is considered in determining his grade for the semester. The director and the student frequently work out sets of goals. These goals will vary according to the performance level of the individual student at the beginning of the term. Modification of objectives may occur as the student progresses. At the conclusion of the semester, the student is graded according to his accomplishment in consideration of his goals. To keep records, the director often uses a card file whereby goals are listed for each student and evaluations are made periodically as the semester progresses.

3. Evaluation in Comparison with a Musical Standard

In this plan, the student strives to reach a predetermined musical standard. Items such as tone, intonation, and musicianship are among those considered in evaluating the student's musical growth during the year. The concept of the musical standard to be achieved may be set forth by the teacher through his own performance on an instrument or by the use of records.

You will probably find that your cooperating teacher uses a combination of the preceding factors in grading the members of the instrumental music class or organization. Other points, such as attendance at extra rehearsals and performances, are also frequently considered in grading.

Evaluating the Performing Organization

You will be somewhat limited in evaluating the results of your work with the performing organization. However, you should be aware of some of the criteria used in the adjudication of the orchestra and band in contests, festivals, and clinics. Objective evaluation of the instrumental organization is attempted through the use of rating scales based upon the following items:

1. Tone: beauty, blend, control.
2. Intonation: chords, melodic line, tutti.
3. Technique: articulation, bowing facility, rhythm.
4. Balance: ensemble, sectional.
5. Interpretation: expression, phrasing, style, tempo.

6. Musical effect: artistry, fluency

7. Other factors: choice of music, instrumentation, discipline, appearance

In the evaluation of your own students, perhaps one of the most difficult phases is that of learning to distinguish degrees of improvement. Since you hear your students daily you are in danger of becoming "deaf" to their performance. The fact that you remember how the students sounded at the beginning of the semester may cause you to be influenced in judging the organization's later sound. As a result, you may become satisfied with your teaching method and may fall into a less then effective teaching routine. To maintain perspective, hear comparable students from other schools as they perform in contests, festivals, and clinics. Also, do not overlook the value of the tape recorder in adding objectivity to the evaluation of the rehearsal or the performance.

Evaluating Planning and Teaching

Improvement in teaching the instrumental class is greatly dependent upon your ability to evaluate, with the assistance of the cooperating teacher and the college supervisor, the effectiveness of both lesson planning and class presentation. For this reason space should be left at the end of each lesson plan form so that notes may be written, following the presentation, concerning the effectiveness of your teaching plan. Recommendations for future lessons should also be included in the written form.

For the purpose of evaluation, schedule periodic conferences with both your cooperating teacher and your college supervisor. You will find that evaluation is a continual process in observing, in planning, and in teaching.

Compilation of Materials

During the student teaching term, keep a record of materials used at your assignment. The gathering of materials is an endless process for a teacher.

List for future reference music, films, records, and other items. A card file is frequently used for this purpose. Included on each reference card are: the complete name of the composition, the composer and arranger, the publisher's name, the price of the item, a description of the composition, suggested grade level, and possible uses of the selection. A reference card should be made for each work performed by the organization and for all materials available in the school music library at your student teaching assignment. A list of films, recordings, books, and periodicals should also be included in the compilation of materials.

Suggestions For Further Reading

Dougless, C. William, "Chamber Music for the Musically Gifted," *Music Educators Journal*, LIII, No. 5 (1967), 95.

Duvall, W. Clyde, *The High School Band Director's Handbook*. Englewood Cliffs, N.J.: Prentice-Hall, Inc., 1962.

Galamian, Ivan, *Principles of Violin Playing and Teaching*. Englewood Cliffs, N.J.: Prentice-Hall, Inc., 1962.

Goldman, Richard Franko, *The Wind Band: Its Literature and Technique*. Boston: Allyn and Bacon, Inc., 1961, Chapters 3, 4, and 5.

Green, Elizabeth A. H., *The Modern Conductor* (2nd ed.). Englewood Cliffs, N.J.: Prentice-Hall, Inc., 1969.

House, Robert W., *Instrumental Music in Today's Schools*. Englewood Cliffs, N.J.: Prentice-Hall, Inc., 1964, Chapters 3, 4, 5, and 6.

———, "Developing An Educative Setting for Performing Groups," *Music Educators Journal*, LIII, No. 1 (1966) 54-56, 144-149.

Lehman, Paul R., *Tests and Measurements in Music*. Englewood Cliffs, N.J.: Prentice-Hall, Inc., 1968.

Levy, Edward, "To Analyze Music, Sketch It," *Music Educators Journal*, LV, No. 5 (1969) 39-40, 117-118.

Thomson, William, "The Ensemble Director and Musical Concepts," *Music Educators Journal*, LIV, No. 9 (1968) 44-46.

Weerts, Richard, "The Beginning Instrumental Program in Perspective," *The Instrumentalist*, XXIII, No. 2 (1968) 46-47.

4

Planning and Teaching: Choral Music

The extent of involvement with the actual conducting of the choirs in your cooperating school will depend on the school level, the types of choirs in the schedule, and the number of concert performances scheduled. Your acquaintance with the choir program during the initial observation period should have shown you that your ego need not be deflated nor your enthusiasm dulled by the fact that the cooperating teacher cannot give you rehearsal responsibility in the form of conducting the advanced choir.

A consideration of scheduling at various levels will remind you of the variety of types, size, and rehearsal schedules which you may find. In the elementary school, the choir may meet several times weekly, either during the school day or before or after school hours. The choir may vary in size from thirty to more than one hundred children and may include boys, girls, or a combination of both. The children may be selected on the basis of musical ability or by their music interest only. The junior high school choral program may include boys, girls, and mixed choirs. As in the elementary school, the advanced junior high school choir usually includes students from the upper grade of the school. Selected by audition, the number of choirs depends upon the size of the school and the strength of the music program. The size of the choirs may vary from thirty to over one hundred and fifty students. In the senior high school, choirs of similar vocal combinations prevail. However, in addition to the advanced organizations, you may find other groups, called variously: training choir, glee club, general chorus, "B" choir, and choral class. While the goals, and subsequently, the morale of the advanced choir are effected by the honor of membership and the activities of the organization, there is generally a variance in the objectives of the other choirs.

The difference in the performance schedule in various levels lies in the number and types of concerts given. The performances of the elementary school choir may include programs for school assembly and parents. The junior high school advanced choir may work toward several performances, including school assemblies, parents' programs, and a festival, clinic or contest. The senior high school advanced choir performances may include school assemblies and evening concerts, service club programs, musicals, clinic-contests, festivals and graduation programs. On the other hand, the less advanced choirs in both junior and senior high school may perform only once or twice during the year since the goals of the training choir or glee club place less emphasis on performance and more on the development of concepts of musical skill and the art of listening.

In the elementary school your involvement in the choir rehearsals may be extensive. In the secondary school you may begin your teaching by working with less advanced choirs, although you may, upon occasion, have the opportunity to conduct section rehearsals and vocal ensembles from the advanced choir. As your experience and ability grow, assignments with the advanced choir may increase.

Whether you are in full command of the choir rehearsal or learning through the work of the cooperating teacher, professional growth will depend upon active involvement in the situation. Involvement is manifested in many ways other than standing before the choir practicing your conducting. The suggestions given here may be utilized in all instances, whether you have limited or extensive opportunity for the actual conducting of the choir:

1. Obtain copies of the choral music used in your assignment for your personal reference library.

2. Analyze the music, marking in your score entrances, important parts for balancing chords, phrasing, pronounciations, and problem phrases as identified by the cooperating teacher and your own analysis.

3. Think through, as time permits, each rehearsal step. Compare your procedure with that of your cooperating teacher.

4. Identify problems. Try to anticipate the cooperating teacher's solution to the problems.

5. Plan the next rehearsal without consulting your cooperating teacher. Then compare your plan with his procedure.

6. Learn the music thoroughly. Staying behind the choir, unobtrusively practice your conducting of the music. Also, practice before a mirror. (It could happen that the cooperating teacher may be ill or unexpectedly called away. Through such practice, you may be prepared to take over the rehearsal.)

7. At times, with your cooperating teacher's approval, move among the various sections. Listen to individual voices. Check the individual accuracy of the vocal parts.

8. Since it is natural that you tend to read most easily and listen most closely to the part you usually sing, practice reading and listening to other sections. This practice may help you to become more proficient in hearing several parts, rather than a single musical line.

9. During your student teaching term, try-outs may occur. They may be for the selection of advanced choir members, for the formation of small ensembles, or for solo parts in a musical or opera. As the cooperating teacher conducts the try-outs you should make your own judgments, later checking and discussing your decisions with his.

10. Whatever the time of day—before or after school or in the evening—you should attend section rehearsals, ensemble practice, try-outs, or any other activity conducted by the cooperating teacher, participating to the greatest possible extent in his schedule. (The extra time will help to demonstrate your sincere interest in the teaching profession and your eagerness to learn from the cooperating teacher. On the other hand, the extra hours necessary to the complete secondary advanced choir program may lead you to decide to enter another profession!)

The above suggestions are but an extension of those given in the discussion of observation in Chapter 2. Most important, you should have a feeling of active participation. If not, some action is needed. Consult with your cooperating teacher and college supervisor; they may recommend additional procedures to fit your particular situation.

Organization of the Rehearsal

In organizing a choir rehearsal, these factors are basic, regardless of the level of type of choir: clearly stated objectives, the selection of materials, the sequence of their presentation, the method of their projection, and the evaluation of the rehearsal. When assigned to conduct a rehearsal, you should prepare a plan for the cooperating teacher's approval. Your goals should be consistent with those of the cooperating teacher. If allowed to select the music, you should obtain the cooperating teacher's approval of your selection (s) even before making the rehearsal plan. Whatever the materials, they must be presented in logical sequence. In choosing the materials, consider these questions: Is the material of musical and educational value? Does the music chosen allow for a change of pace by providing varying moods, tempo, dynamic level and general difficulty? Are special vocalises to be used at the beginning of the rehearsal? Are the vocalises directly concerned with the music of the rehearsal period? Is new music always presented before review, or is there variance from day to day depending upon the needs of the choir? How can the study of music history and theory be coordinated with the rehearsal music? Is time allowed for sight reading? How is the organization of materials different in the elementary, junior and senior high schools? How is it similar?

Having selected the materials for the rehearsal, you are now ready to organize your rehearsal plan. Through observation you will have recognized the need for careful planning and, also, the necessity for departing from the lesson plan as the situation dictates. Even though the procedure may be changed during the rehearsal, the fact that you have taken time to establish goals and to study the material of the rehearsal will help you to give your total attention to working with the pupils.

Basic to successful planning is sensitivity to the needs of the pupils. A real challenge lies in the opportunity to plan for choirs of various advancement levels. However, the basic musical experiences of the choir rehearsal vary little in moving from elementary to junior and senior high school levels. The difference lies in the amount of time given to each organization, the allotment of time within the period, the sophistication of the materials used, and the maturity level of the pupils. The secondary school choir usually meets more often than the elementary school choir, and the rehearsal periods are generally longer. Modular and other types of flexible scheduling may allow for irregular rehearsal periods and, in some instances, extended rehearsal time for both individual pupils and choir. Certainly, the choir meeting daily and for longer periods may learn more music than that having two or three rehearsals weekly. Too, the attention span grows as the students mature. However, the same ingredients are necessary for all levels: clearly stated goals, a variety of materials, a logical presentation of the materials, and proper pacing of the rehearsal.

Study various approaches to the elementary and secondary advanced and training choir rehearsal plans, noting the differences. These differences relate not only to difficulty of materials but also to the distribution of time within the rehearsal. You may wish to organize and try several plans for the presentation of the same material. Development of skill in such creativity serves to increase the flexibility necessary for successful planning and teaching.

Several lesson plan examples are presented here to help you in planning for your teaching. You will find it better to plan for extra rather than for insufficient material. This means that no time is wasted in issuing extra music after the rehearsal has started. Planning ahead for extra material also provides the flexibility necessary for the unexpected rehearsal interruptions, the particular mood of the pupils, and other factors which affect the rehearsal periods. Including suggested time for each part of the rehearsal should help to avoid spending too much time in any one phase.

The plan in Figure 4-1 would change format in the rehearsals immediately preceding a concert performance in that the introduction of new material would give way to the refinement of the entire program. The warm-up time and the summation should remain, and a time for motivation—restatement of goals and a generation of interest and pride in the up-coming performance—should be added.

The secondary school rehearsal is usually of longer duration. The plan in Figure 4-2 points up differences made necessary by the maturity level. The increased time allows for the presentation of more material. The motivation in the introduction of a new song and the summation may be more concise, requiring less time than that suggested in the elementary choir rehearsal plan.

REHEARSAL PLAN: ELEMENTARY SCHOOL CHOIR

Objectives To continue emphasis on correct singing habits
To introduce a new song
To refine the performance of a learned song

Procedure

Attendance check, music distribution, announcements (regular
routine) 5%

Warm-up 10%
Emphasis on correct breathing.
Emphasis on vowel sounds (using words from song text to il-
lustrate and practice.)

Introduce new song 40%
Sing or play recording of the song as children follow score
Discuss song: composer, text, background, style (use both
lecture and question methods to motivate interest)
Have choir sight sing, with or without piano
Work on individual parts in beginning section of song

Continue refinement of previously learned song(s) 30%-35%
Remind choir of previous rehearsal's accomplishment.
Sing as needed for final polishing.

Review learned song(s) chosen by children if time permits.

Summation of rehearsal 10%-15%
Objective questions directed to entire choir and individual
children re: warm-up and new song
Praise accomplishment
Point out work necessary in next rehearsal
Put away materials

Evaluation

Figure 4-1.

```
┌─────────────────────────────────────────────────────────────────────┐
│                                                                       │
│     REHEARSAL PLAN: SECONDARY SCHOOL ADVANCED CHOIR                    │
│                                                                       │
├─────────────────────────────────────────────────────────────────────┤
│                                                                       │
│   Objectives   To introduce a new song                                │
│                To polish the performance of learned song(s)           │
│                To practice sight reading                               │
│                                                                       │
├─────────────────────────────────────────────────────────────────────┤
│                                                                       │
│   Procedure                                                           │
│                                                                       │
│          Attendance check, music distribution, announcements (regular │
│          routine) . . . . . . . . . . . . . . . . . . . .        5%   │
│                                                                       │
│          Vocalises . . . . . . . . . . . . . . . . . . .        10%   │
│          Utilize material of rehearsal music.                         │
│                                                                       │
│          Introduce new song  . . . . . . . . . . . . . . .       40%  │
│          Play entire song on piano (or recording) as choir follows score │
│          Discuss composer and style of the music                      │
│          Choir sings entire song                                      │
│          Work on parts as needed                                      │
│                                                                       │
│          Review learned song(s) for polishing performance  . . . . .  20% │
│                                                                       │
│          Sight reading . . . . . . . . . . . . . . . . . .       15%  │
│                                                                       │
│          Conclude rehearsal . . . . . . . . . . . . . . . .      10%  │
│          Summation of accomplishment, pointing to work of next re-    │
│          hearsal                                                      │
│          Announcements by choir officers                              │
│          Putting away music                                           │
│                                                                       │
├─────────────────────────────────────────────────────────────────────┤
│                                                                       │
│   Evaluation                                                          │
│                                                                       │
└─────────────────────────────────────────────────────────────────────┘
```

Figure 4-2.

A study of Figure 4-2 shows emphasis on several factors:

1. Minimum time is given to class routine at the beginning of the rehearsal.

2. The vocalises require a short time and are directed to the rehearsal music rather than to isolated objectives.

3. Variety in the musical activities is provided.

4. In introducing a new song, attention is given to composer, style, etc.

5. The director ends the rehearsal in a positive manner.

6. The officers are given recognition.

7. Following the rehearsal, the director, in the evaluation section, notes the particular success of some techniques and the need for altering others.

The training choir is of great value in the development and maintenance of an effective secondary choral program. It provides not only a vehicle for the nurture of individual pupil talent but it also serves as the terminal musical experience for many students. Consequently, it is important to plan for activities such as music history, basic theory and learning how to listen to music along with singing. This program is especially important when general music courses are not included in the curriculum.

For example, on Monday, Wednesday, and Friday the teacher might devote the primary portion of the class time to vocal activities, for which the plan in Figure 4-3 may serve as a guide.

REHEARSAL PLAN: SECONDARY SCHOOL TRAINING CHOIR (MWF)

Objectives To guide individual pupils in acquiring skill in vocal production
To further pupils' musical skill
To increase the choral repertoire

Procedure

Attendance check, music distribution, announcements (regular routine) 5%

Vocal production study: breath control exercises and vocalises or simple songs 20%

Musicianship study: 25%
Interval drill—aural and oral
Study of notation, key signatures, etc.
Sight singing

Introduction of new song 30%

Review of previously learned song(s) 15%

Conclusion:
Summation and putting away materials 5%

Evaluation

Figure 4-3.

The Tuesday and Thursday class periods for the training choir may be based on the music introduced in the choral rehearsals of Monday, Wednesday, and Friday. Suggested activities for those classes include: study of the composers, listening to recordings of other music by the composers whose works are sung, study of music styles, and conducting familiar music. Planning for these lessons is similar to the organization of the general music class, which will be discussed in Chapter 5.

Another approach to the organization of the training choir is to combine the two types of activities within the class period. Both plans of organization may be used before deciding which is more appropriate for your situation. Regardless of the plan selected, singing experiences may be organized into units such as those discussed in Chapter 5.

Presentation

The projection of the rehearsal plan into a meaningful presentation is your next task. It is not only impossible, but it would be detrimental to try to write into the plan every word to be spoken. Occasionally, oral practice of the presentation may be helpful. For example, it may be beneficial to practice conducting before a mirror. In the same vein, the lesson plan can only indicate the direction of your procedure for guiding the pupils in achieving an awareness of aural concepts such as correct vocal tone, pitch and singing in tune. You will find that your success in balancing the vocal parts to achieve the correct total effect is directly related to your own and your pupils' sensitivity to this area of singing.

Before every rehearsal, study your score so thoroughly that you are free to make eye contact with the individual choir members as you rehearse the group. Sensitivity to the members of the organization helps you to know when students have memorized the music, when their reactions indicate individual problems in the music, and when they become bored. If the vocal score is to be used in the rehearsal, keep it at a height that will allow you to view the members of the choir. Feel free to leave the podium and to move among the various sections as they rehearse vocal parts, thereby allowing you an opportunity to hear individual voices. If you conduct the rehearsal from the piano, place the instrument directly in front of the choir. By placing the music on top of the piano and standing, or sitting on a high stool you can keep eye contact with the group. During the early stages of rehearsing the vocal parts, conducting is generally unnecessary. After the choir has mastered the music and text, begin conducting as you work with the students to achieve a refined performance.

Since the choir members must learn to depend upon their own musicality, you should avoid singing with the choir. Even more important is the fact that you cannot hear the choir when you sing or when you use the piano indiscriminately. Wise use of the piano is an important factor in the choir rehearsal, but dependence on it should be avoided. Be aware of the fact that individual voice parts are never really mastered until they are sung easily without accompaniment. Likewise, constant reference to the piano for a pitch results in lazy rehearsal habits. If encouraged and challenged by the director, choirs at all levels can develop proficiency and gain musical satisfaction by maintaining tonality and recalling pitches without the aid of the piano.

Rehearsal time is often wasted in the misuse of vocalises. Used functionally with the rehearsal music, they have value; performed aimlessly with no relation to the music, they are worthless. Carefully consider the amount of time allowed for vocalizing material and, of even more importance, whether the vocalises are effecting a change in the vocal sound of the choir. Students of all levels are capable of achieving results when they understand the reason for the vocalises. You should understand thoroughly the purpose of the vocalises before using them. For example, the use of a vocalise sung in your college choir does not necessarily make it correct for your pupils. According to the situation, a vocalise may be suitable for one group or time and completely useless in another.

To project your concept of the desired choral tone, plan to use recordings of other choirs. You may also use your own voice, not to be imitated, but rather to demonstrate correct vocal production. Regardless of the age level or advancement of the choir, the director's primary objective is to develop a unified and pleasing tonal concept. Sharing your objectives and reasons for procedures with your pupils makes for faster realization of your goals. For instance, basic exercises for breath control may seem tedious to young students unless the reasons for them are understood and unless they are presented logically. Once the desired tone is achieved, the type of vocalise used is adapted to other objectives, such as flexibility and increase of vocal range, or as vocal warm-ups.

Included in your early rehearsal plans will be the introduction of a new composition. The method used generally depends upon the age level and advancement of the choir, the difficulty of the music, and the psychological effect desired by the director. The choir's early understanding of the performance style of the music, as intended by the composer, often facilitates the learning process. On the other hand, an extended lecture on the theoretical difficulties to be encountered may destroy much of the potential interest in the music. An effective method of introducing a new composition is to:

1. Play it on the piano or play a recording if available.
2. Have the choir sing the entire number, either accompanied or a cappella.
3. Isolate and rehearse difficult parts.
4. Combine parts.

The thorough mastery of vocal parts is necessary for a good performance. The problem of being thorough in the learning of the parts without boring the choir presents a formidable challenge. One method of accomplishing this is to maintain the stylistic interpretation of the music even during the learning of parts. At the same time, identify and also encourage the choir members to identify the musical difficulties encountered by various sections. As individual parts are rehearsed, avoid extensive drill on simple parts. Combine parts as quickly as possible, making sure the students are musically secure. Because of the variance in choral music and because of the difference in the learning ability of students, it is impossible to set guidelines for the order of combining the vocal parts. Each composition presents different problems. However, you will want to involve all students as much as possible to avoid boredom and ensuing discipline problems. An effective technique is to have the entire choir sing the particular problem phrase or group of notes with the section having difficulty.

It is vital, as you continue to work with the choir, that your ability to identify and solve performance problems grows. It is important to hear errors and to recognize instantly in which section they are made. Rather than having the entire choir repeat the music, you may isolate the measure or phrase and work with the section having difficulty. For instance, if the soprano section has difficulty on page five of the music, the drill should begin on that page or at the beginning of the phrase, not on page one of the music.

Along with awareness of where the problem is, you must recognize what it is. For example, difficulty in singing one note, perhaps an accidental, may not relate to that single pitch but to the preceding note or notes. Sometimes the problem is caused by faulty rhythms. A few minutes spent in speaking the words in tempo or tapping the rhythm usually produces more effective results than repeated singing of the passage. In another instance, poor intonation may be due to faulty tone production.

After the parts are learned, you and the choir should continue striving to perfect the expressive elements of the music. The practice of having the high school choir memorize the music varies among directors. Study the following theories. First, memorizing the music frees the choir from the printed page and allows for complete attention to the director. Too, the performance is enhanced by the absence of distracting vocal scores. Since memorizing skill improves through practice, many directors include this requirement as a necessary goal for their choirs. The second theory holds that the use of the score in performance saves rehearsal time, thereby allowing the development of a larger repertoire than possible when the music is memorized. The use of the score, it is thought, sometimes lessens the tension of the choir members by serving as a crutch for note and text recall. However, you may discover that by the time a choir has mastered the vocal and interpretive problems of the composition, the music will be practically memorized. It is advisable to expect the elementary and junior high school choirs to memorize their music because their limited experience generally precludes their skilled handling of a score during a performance. The two theories concerning the choir's memorizing of music pertain also to the director's use of a score. Since the ability to memorize a complete score improves with practice, you should give consideration to developing this skill. Certainly, the final polishing of the music depends upon the director's complete command of the score.

One aid to the refinement of the performance is the use of a tape recorder which allows the students to evaluate their progress and to analyze their problems in diction, phrasing, tone quality, balance and dynamics. Also, hearing a recording of a professional choir's singing the music may be an effective factor in the polishing of the performance.

The point at which the director considers the composition finished depends upon his knowledge of the musical ability of the students, his judgment of their performance readiness, the date scheduled for the performance of the music, and the time necessary for "seasoning". The "seasoning" period may vary in length from days to weeks. It may mean that the choir works on other music and returns to the performance numbers for short review only occasionally. This period of time allows the choir to have a command of the music not possible when the performance follows immediately upon the learning.

Elementary School Choir

As noted in the rehearsal plan for the elementary school choir, time for the practice of sight reading was not included. The reason for the omission is that this choir is not a substitute for the general music program, but rather, an adjunct. Since the rehearsal time is limited and the calling of extra rehearsals is less than desirable, full time should be given to learning the song material, leaving the practice of sight reading for the general music class included in the children's daily schedule. Often the choir meets for rehearsal before the beginning of the school day, placing upon parents a large responsibility for helping their children to make the early rehearsals. You should, therefore, be in the rehearsal room, with the rehearsal set-up arranged, 15-30 minutes before the appointed time. Begin promptly, whether all the children are there or not. You should maintain the highest expectation of attention from the children during the rehearsal; it is helpful to allow them to relax in their chairs when not singing, sitting forward in an attitude of alertness when singing. Standing for brief times is advisable, also. The same procedure is necessary regardless of the time of the rehearsal. In fact, in the rehearsal held during the school schedule but in the afternoon, you may find need for more changes of position—sitting, standing—in that children tend to become tired and restless as the school day nears its closing time.

In selecting songs for the choir, use several sources: the adopted series books, song collections, and choral octavos. Although the series books include suitable material, psychologically there is an advantage in choosing other sources since the children work in the series books in their general music classes. The opportunity to include art songs in the children's repertoire is offered through unison singing. The blending of the voices and the projection of the spirit and meaning of the text necessary for beautiful unison singing should provide a satisfying musical experience for you and the children. The elementary school choir may also sing songs of two and three parts. If you have the opportunity to teach more than one song, first teach a two-part or descant song, then proceed to the more intricate three parts. A problem in teaching a part song is keeping the other children involved while one section learns a part. Some suggestions for the teaching of part songs are given here:

1. Have all sections rhythm read both in neutral syllables and in words.
2. Work with individual sections for very short periods.
3. While working with one section, have other children follow this part. Ask for their suggestions, identifying and solving problems, as you work.
4. Avoid dependence on the piano and your own singing in teaching parts.
5. Demand perfection in learning parts. It is difficult, even impossible, for children to correct notes learned incorrectly in the beginning.
6. Praise and encourage the children regularly as they work on the music.

The limited rehearsals for the elementary choir demand maximum use of time. Your skill, in your cooperating teacher's judgment, will determine the extent of your involvement with the choir. As you prepare to work with the elementary choir, review the suggestions concerning discipline in Chapter 2. Your observation of the children in your cooperating school will have helped you to judge their capacity for learning, their habits of attentiveness, their interest in music, and their over-all attitudes. Success depends greatly on the climate established in your first one or two rehearsals. Correcting a poor beginning is time-consuming and difficult. Discipline problems often arise through the director's behavior. The fact that you are working with what is usually, in the elementary school, a selected honor group only indicates the need for greater challenging of the children on your part. To meet this challenge, you must move quickly through the rehearsal, avoiding waits and hesitations. At the first sign of inattention prepare to change the material or the procedure, or both. As a student teacher you have little opportunity for entering into teacher-pupil planning of the year's activities. However, you should share with the children, throughout the rehearsal, the goals for the day as set forth in your introduction of the rehearsal. Children need to be reminded, more often than older pupils, of their goals. At the same time, they need and will respond to your assurance of their progress toward these goals. Or, if they slack off, use the goals as a positive, rather than negative, means of encouraging more effort on their part. Finally, make time in your planning for the children to sing songs of their own choosing. As a student teacher acquaint yourself with the music they have previously learned.

Junior High School Choir

Whatever the grade distribution in your cooperating school—6, 7, 8;   7, 8, 9;   7, 8, or other—the primary problem is the selection of music suitable for the changing voices of this age level. No college methods class or textbook can prepare you adequately for the perplexities of the adolescent voice. Follow your cooperating teacher's suggestions in choosing music. The same organization as suggested for the elementary school will be necessary. You should review the ideas presented in that section. You will probably find that this group offers a different kind of challenge in that they are more aware of what they want and they place more responsibility on their teachers to provide necessary leadership. You will have observed the tendency to inconsistency of behavior of these children from day to day. They may, at times, outwardly appear to challenge your teaching and to test your ability. Several factors will help you in meeting this challenge:

1. Thorough advance preparation for your rehearsal (written plan, study of and practice for the presentation).
2. A show of self-confidence (not to be confused with arrogance) in your first and second rehearsals.
3. Effective pacing of the rehearsal, with no obvious indecision as to your next step.
4. Consistency in your attitude: firmness, good humor, emotional control.

Again, as in the elementary choir, effectiveness in the early rehearsals enhances the possibility for a successful experience in student teaching. However, you should continue to build on this early success. If efforts are relaxed, even in the smallest degree, you may experience difficulty. Your goal should be to make continuous progress in stimulating your pupils' musical growth.

Senior High School Choir

By this time, you realize that the basic ingredients for choir rehearsals of all types and levels are similar: the rehearsal set-up must be pre-arranged, the written plan must be completed, the presentation must be practiced, and the evaluation must follow each rehearsal. The difference lies in the difficulty of the material and the ability of the pupils. In the senior high school, asking the training choir and general chorus to sing very difficult music totally discourages the pupils. At the same time, too much easy music stifles the growth and interest of the advanced choir.

As has been stated, you will probably have more opportunity to work with the training choir than with the advanced choir. The same principles of teaching apply to these pupils as to young children. For instance, they may become bored, in spite of their longer attention span, with your presentation. If bored, they may very likely "turn off" their inner initiative to learn, even while displaying an outward attitude of cooperation with you. This cooperative attitude generally prevails in the senior high school: if you are an effective student teacher, the pupils are pleased. If you are less than proficient, or even totally ineffective, these pupils often tend to feel sympathetic toward you, often to the point of trying to help you to appear effective during the visits of your college supervisor. Your self-evaluation and that of your cooperating teacher and college supervisor will be especially important in helping you to know whether your teaching is truly effective or is merely being tolerated by the pupils. A related factor in working with senior high school pupils is that their maturity, closeness to your own age, and their ability to imagine themselves in your place add to a greater tolerance for and interest in you, personally. Even though your first inclination is to accept and reciprocate their friendliness, you should maintain a proper teacher-pupil relationship at all times.

The suggestions for teaching parts in the elementary and junior high school choirs and also in the presentation section of this chapter should be reviewed. The difference in the music of these various levels lies in its complexity. Ability to hear four to eight parts in "depth" will require long, continuous experience.

Evaluation

Opportunity to evaluate your pupils' progress in choral music may be quite limited at this point. However, several techniques are available and useful to you as you seek to evaluate your own growth:

1. Completion of the daily rehearsal evaluation included in your rehearsal plan.
2. Regular use of tape recording of rehearsal.
3. Use of video tape of rehearsal.
4. Suggestions of cooperating teacher and college supervisor for improvement in rehearsal techniques.

Even though you are not engaged in conducting the choir in competition the use of standard rating forms by the cooperating teacher and college supervisor in helping to evaluate your performance with the choir would be valuable for your progress as well as to acquaint you with the rating procedure.

As has been pointed out, evaluation is a continuing process and requires the ability to give and to receive criticism. Willingness to seek and to accept evaluation and then to alter procedures as this evaluation shows advisable is important evidence of probable future success as a choral director.

Suggestions For Further Reading

Cooper, Irvin, and Karl O. Kuersteiner, Teaching Junior High School Music. *Boston: Allyn and Bacon, Inc., 1967, Chapters 6 and 10.*

Ehmann, Wilhelm, Choral Directing. *Minneapolis, Minn.: Augsburg Publishing House, 1968, Section B: Chapters 1, 4, and 5.*

Garretson, Robert L., Conducting Choral Music. *Boston: Allyn and Bacon, Inc., 1963, Chapters 1, 2, 3, and 4.*

Knauf, Robert, "Junior High School—The Pivotal Point," in Choral Director's Guide, eds. Kenneth L. Neidig and John W. Jennings. *West Nyack, New York: Parker Publishing Co., Inc., 1967, Chapter 9.*

Larson, Le Roy, "More Than Performance: It Can Be Done," Music Educators Journal, *1969.*

Lawson, Warner, "Practical Rehearsal Techniques," Choral Director's Guide, eds. Kenneth L. Neidig and John W. Jennings. *West Nyack, N. Y.: Parker Publishing Co., Inc., 1967, Chapter 11.*

Leonhard, Charles, and Robert W. House, Foundations and Principles of Music Education. *New York: McGraw-Hill Book Company, 1959, p. 211-215.*

Lukin, Laszlo, "The Teaching of Singing and Music in Primary and Secondary School," Musical Education in Hungary, ed. Frigges Sandor. *Budapest: Cowina Press, 1966, pp 109-134.*

McElheran, Brock, Conducting Technique. *New York: Oxford University Press, 1966, Chapters 3 and 21.*

Nordholm, Harriet, Singing in the Elementary Schools. *Englewood Cliffs, N. J.: Prentice-Hall, Inc., 1966, pp. 77-79.*

Pfautsch, Lloyd, Mental Warmups for the Choral Conductor. *New York: Lawson-Gould, 1969.*

Sur, William R., and Charles F. Schuller, Music Education For Teen-Agers. *New York: Harper & Row, Publishers, 1966, Chapters 5 and 12.*

5

Planning and Teaching: General Music

Observation of the general music program will have shown you the variations in the scheduling of classes. In the elementary school the children may participate in a music class several times a week or daily. In the junior high school the status of the class—whether required or an elective—will be of concern to you. Usually, general music is an elective in the senior high school. Consider this an advantage in that the pupils have chosen the course. However, you will find that in some instances the pupils elected the course only as a last resort. In this case planning must involve "selling" music to these students. If the general music classes in your cooperating school are involved in a humanities program, you may have the opportunity to participate in team teaching with art, social studies, and language arts teachers.

Organizing Materials

Because the scope of general music activities is so extensive, it is a problem in teaching to decide where to begin. The experienced teacher knows that ideas used in previous years' classes may be totally ineffective for the current year and must therefore be adapted or changed for each group. Study the materials available to the cooperating teacher. In the elementary school the basic materials for general music may be taken from one or more of the contemporary music series books. The junior and senior high school teacher may refer to curriculum guides and other references for aid in the selection of materials. However, in both instances, the organization of the material must be planned by the teacher and the pupils. Some considerations in the selection of materials for the class are:

1. The age and maturity level of the pupils

2. The quality of the music

3. The use of materials which are attractive to the pupils

4. Variety in the materials, such as films, filmstrips and other resource material

5. The past experience of the pupils

Materials for the general music course include song books, recordings, maps, charts, films, filmstrips, and social studies, art and language arts resource material.

The enrichment of the general music course is dependent on the teacher's interest in and knowledge of other areas such as history, literature, philosophy and the arts. The inter-relatedness of the program depends on several factors: the interests of the pupils individually and as a group, the curriculum structure in the school, and the teacher's experience and interest.

As you organize the materials to be used, study the pupil-centered learning situation created by the cooperating teacher, how the pupils participate in the situation, and how this procedure prevents problems in class control. Although the word "interest" has been over-used, it is still significant in planning for musical growth. It is definitely more advisable to stop an activity at the peak of the pupils' interest than to continue past the climax of the learning period. The pupil-centered situation involves creativity, a term often misunderstood. While creativeness demands individual thinking, it does not imply undisciplined action. It occurs when pupils, with the teacher's leadership, work individually and collectively to attain certain goals. Note the cooperating teacher's success in this type of teaching and prepare your lessons so that you may attain maximum student participation. You should understand that a basic factor in encouraging pupils to this maximum participation is the quality, not the quantity, of the activities in the general music class.

The cooperating teacher will probably have established long-range goals—six or nine weeks or a semester. As a student teacher, you will generally be working in the day-by-day planning of immediate goals. For example, a seventh grade unit might be based upon a study of American music. The long range objectives may be to give pupils an overview of the development of music in America, and to become acquainted with the music of early and contemporary composers. Immediate goals may include:

1. learning American folk songs.

2. learning about the music of early American settlers

3. learning songs of American composers

4. becoming familiar with instrumental music—band, orchestra and ensemble—of American composers

5. learning early American singing games, rhythms and square dances.

Setting these and other goals up through coordinated planning gives the teacher and pupils the opportunity to know where they are going and what they will have accomplished at the conclusion of the unit. In setting up both long-range and immediate goals, you should be aware that it is necessary to include time for review. The student teacher is frequently shocked to find that a lesson cannot be mastered and retained after a single exposure. Review not only helps the pupil to retain information but also serves as a sequential link from one learning concept to another.

As in choral and instrumental music, the need for a logical arrangement and presentation is vital. Without continuity, materials will have little or no meaning for your pupils. During observation of your cooperating teacher you will become aware of both the continuity of the materials presented and the teacher's recognition of the pupil's need in determining this continuity. The organization of the material into units or projects often serves to give direction to the pupils' learning. As a guide to the types of units to be used, you may draw upon the subject matter of history, language arts and other areas. In some elementary schools, the entire school curriculum is coordinated. For instance, if the study of Russia is included in the social studies, the literature, art and music are presented by the respective area teachers, as in the core curriculum or team teaching situation. Units based on the study of music—form, rhythm, instrumentation, and others—should also be included.

Lesson Planning

As in instrumental and choral music, the teaching phase follows your observation period. You will have had the opportunity to study the cooperating teacher's approach to the teaching of general music and to observe the pupils in the various classes. Toward the conclusion of the observation period, you should plan your first lesson or lessons. The first lesson may be part of a larger unit previously developed by the cooperating teacher, or it may consist of a one lesson presentation, complete in itself. Your cooperating teacher may assign the lesson and unit topics and suggest the musical materials to be used for your first lesson, or he may give you complete freedom in choosing a subject area. In either case, have your lesson plan approved by the cooperating teacher and, in some instances, your college supervisor before your presentation.

As a guide to planning your lessons in all levels, these suggestions are given:

1. Good planning includes active involvement of the pupils.

2. Good planning allows flexibility.

3. Good planning follows the goals of the course.

4. Good planning includes careful thinking through the written plan outline before the oral presentation.

5. Good planning insures that there is a logical moving from one lesson to another.

6. Good planning includes a variety of teaching procedures.

Basic to the planning for teaching general music is the need to arrange the class activities to include singing, listening, moving, and playing. While it may be unwise to attempt the four activities in one lesson, they should be included within the weekly general music curriculum. In planning, variety is a necessity. For instance, if an entire lesson is devoted to questions and answers about one song, the result for you and your pupils may be utter boredom.

Although you may have had no opportunity to enter into the cooperating teacher's over-all plan, study it and make sure your short-term plans for the day and week contribute to the semester plan. Many approaches to lesson plans may be used. Try more than one before forming an opinion on the merit of a particular plan.

From your earlier work in college methods classes you will have been exposed to the formulation of lesson plans. Although there may be variations in the general style, some elements of the plan are basic and vital. At this time, it may be helpful for you to review these:

   I. Title (opt.)
  II. Time (1 day, 2 days, etc.)
 III. Objective(s)
 IV. Materials
  V. Procedure (activities)
      A. Daily goals
      B. Motivation
      C. Summation
 VI. Evaluation

In preparing the lesson at all levels you may note the approximate time you wish to devote to each phase of the lesson. Many inexperienced teachers consider this unnecessary. However, since the ability to pace the lesson is one of the requisites for effective teaching, include suggested timing for your own guideline. To be sure, it is difficult for an inexperienced student teacher, with little practical knowledge in this area, to make even an estimate. Nevertheless, efforts in formal planning should help you to learn more quickly how to pace your teaching and the importance of considering time in achieving results. Whatever the format make each plan as clear and concise as possible. There are several reasons:

1. Your cooperating teacher and college supervisor can evaluate the plan at a glance.

2. You will be able to refer to it as you prepare and present your lesson.

3. You may use it for your teaching in later years.

The motivation for the lesson is so important that it is often given a main area title in the lesson plan. The effective teacher gains the pupils' attention and interest through effective motivation. "Open your books to page one" as an opening statement seldom heralds an exciting learning experience. In like manner, the lesson which concludes with "pass your books in" probably signifies to the class the welcome ending of a dull period. In other words, devote as much attention to the beginning and closing of the lesson as to the selection of the material. Motivation sets the tone of the day's lesson. The summation provides the opportunity to cement the pupils' learning and satisfaction with the lesson as well as to instigate the motivation for the next day's learning experience.

Included in the procedure should be the logical step-by-step process necessary for attaining the goals of the day. If questions are to be used, they should be specifically stated in your lesson plan. The relevancy of the questions is important to effective teaching. Writing them will help to determine their value in implementing the lesson.

It is vital that you evaluate each lesson in terms of your own and your pupils' response to the lesson. The suggestions of the cooperating teacher and the college supervisor should be included in the evaluation section. At this time, too, note necessary alterations in activities and materials.

Since effective lesson plans will help you to develop superior teaching techniques, it is important that you give much time to their preparation. As your skill in teaching increases, you may include less detail, but the need for organization and planning will remain an absolute necessity.

Elementary (Lower) School Lesson Plans

In your elementary school assignment, you will probably be involved in planning for the teaching of several grade levels. An effective method of beginning the teaching phase is to plan for one class and within a day or two adding other classes of the same grade level, continuing for a week or more before assuming responsibility for another grade level. This sequence of adding classes gradually should be satisfactorily accomplished in approximately fifty to seventy percent of your student teaching term, thereby allowing you to teach all of the classes during the remainder of the term. The guidance of the cooperating teacher and the college supervisor will continue to be of primary importance as you plan for and teach your classes. You should understand, however, that it is not always possible for you to teach all of the classes. Your teaching load will be determined by the cooperating teacher and the college supervisor and will be based upon your ability in relation to the long range goals of the class.

In the elementary school the need for flexibility in lesson planning will be readily apparent as you prepare for two or more classes of the same grade level.

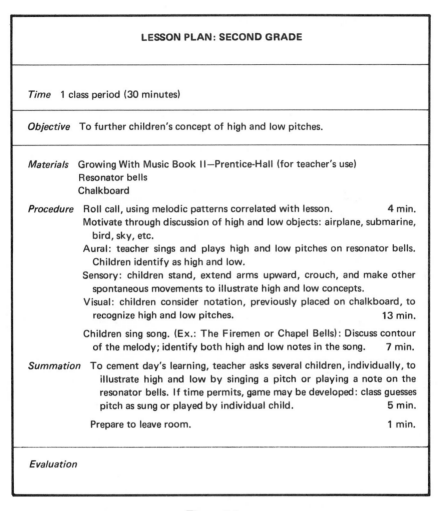

LESSON PLAN: SECOND GRADE

Time　1 class period (30 minutes)

Objective　To further children's concept of high and low pitches.

Materials　Growing With Music Book II—Prentice-Hall (for teacher's use)
Resonator bells
Chalkboard

Procedure　Roll call, using melodic patterns correlated with lesson.　4 min.
Motivate through discussion of high and low objects: airplane, submarine, bird, sky, etc.
Aural: teacher sings and plays high and low pitches on resonator bells. Children identify as high and low.
Sensory: children stand, extend arms upward, crouch, and make other spontaneous movements to illustrate high and low concepts.
Visual: children consider notation, previously placed on chalkboard, to recognize high and low pitches.　13 min.

Children sing song. (Ex.: The Firemen or Chapel Bells): Discuss contour of the melody; identify both high and low notes in the song.　7 min.

Summation　To cement day's learning, teacher asks several children, individually, to illustrate high and low by singing a pitch or playing a note on the resonator bells. If time permits, game may be developed: class guesses pitch as sung or played by individual child.　5 min.

Prepare to leave room.　1 min.

Evaluation

Figure 5-1.

Each group of children will have behavioral and learning patterns which distinguish it from other groups. You may develop a single lesson plan as the basis for several classes, but this plan should be flexible enough to allow you to alter it as the need arises from class to class. Extra material should always be included in your lesson plan. It will help you to adjust to the individual needs of your classes and of individual pupils in each class. At the same time, this extra material will be of use to you in contingencies such as an unexpected extension of the period; the completion of the lesson in less than your anticipated time; or an obvious need to omit a planned song, record, or other material due to the class mood of the day.

After preparing detailed lesson plan, study and master it through practice with a child, a friend, or before a mirror. You may then wish to make a less detailed "cue" card for use during your presentation. It is important that you keep one of these before you; it will help you to overcome the nervousness that usually occurs in the early experience of standing before your pupils.

Also, it will insure including each step of your lesson in a sequential pattern.

The plan in Figure 5-1 includes the basic parts necessary for an effective lesson and is an example of a lesson built on a music concept. Its special value lies in its use as a referral point for future lessons in music reading. A "cue" card for your presentation of this lesson is shown in Figure 5-2.

Procedure Roll call—high, low melodic patterns   4 min.

Motivation: discuss high-low objects.
Aural: sing—play high, low pitches.
Children identify.
Sensory: children create movements to illustrate high-low concept.
Visual: have children identify notation on chalkboard as high-low for
clarity.   13 min.

Children sing song(s): The Fireman, Chapel Bells. Melodic contour—children identify high, low notes in song.   7 min.

Summation Ask individual children to sing or play high-low pitches. Play
identification game.   5 min.

Prepare to leave room.   1 min.

Figure 5-2.

Frequently you will find that it is feasible to coordinate music with social studies in the elementary school. The plan in Figure 5-3 presents an example of this.

The unit offers flexibility in that the activities are not assigned to specific days but may be used in a sequence which evolves logically from the planning of teacher and pupils. For instance, the last activity—committee projects—may provide the impetus for the unit, in which case the committees should be formed on the first day.

**A UNIT FOR FIFTH GRADE: MUSIC OF EARLY AMERICA—
COLONIAL AND REVOLUTIONARY WAR**

Time   2-3 weeks.

Objectives   To acquaint the pupils with their musical heritage.
To show how folk music grows from the daily living of the people.
To acquaint pupils with early American composer, William Billings.

Materials   Birchard Series, Book V
   "Boston Tea Party"
   "In Good Old Colony Times"

Making Music Your Own, Book V—Silver Burdett
   "Blow the Man Down"
   "Hammer Man"
   "Chester"
   "Johnny Has Gone for a Soldier"
   "Chairs to Mend"
   "Old Joe Clark"

"Yankee Doodle"

Record player,
Recording of New England Triptych—Wm. Schuman,

Films depicting early American life,

Instruments: bells, autoharp, piano, rhythm,

Activities   Learn songs (as many of above as desired)
Use instruments with songs
Listen to the recording (correlate with the learning of Chester)
See film(s)
Learn the Virginia Reel (with Old Joe Clark)
Arrange bulletin boards, including maps and pictures of Colonial America
Present oral reports, include poetry of the period
Work in committee projects

Evaluation

Figure 5-3.

Secondary School
Lesson Plans

In spite of various attempts to strengthen the status of general music in secondary schools, there is still such a wide degree of differences in practice that it is difficult to generalize. As a student teacher you may find junior high general music classes given only in the seventh grade. Or you may find it scheduled through the eighth grade from one to five times weekly. If the sixth grade is included in the school, music may be offered only to those pupils. Whatever the curriculum organization, it will be necessary to prepare lesson plans. The class period may be of forty to sixty minutes in length depending upon the type of scheduling. The basis of the lesson plan is identical to that which you prepare in the lower school.

There are both differences and similarities in the two levels. Since the child's attention span increases each year, the length of time for each activity is increased at the junior high school level. There is a need for variety in the materials and activities and in the presentation procedures in both elementary and junior high school. In teacher-pupil planning, the junior high school pupils may be expected to work more effectively in group committee projects than the lower level pupils. More individual research on special music areas can be encouraged in the junior high school than in the elementary school. Older children can derive as much satisfaction out of creating and perfecting a square dance performance as can small children in floating around the room to ballet music or responding to a galloping rhythm. In developing procedure, adapt your language vocabulary and terminology to the maturity level of your pupils. However, at both levels, you should avoid talking down to your pupils.

Since studies show that boys' voices are changing at an earlier age than formerly, choosing song material may be a problem in upper elementary as well as in junior high school general music classes. Before preparing your lesson plan, you should have observed the classes sufficiently to know the pupils' voice ranges and capabilities. You may need to add a vocal part of only two or three notes for one or more boys. To provide a satisfying singing experience, you may wish to transpose the song (s) for unison singing. Such problems must be noted as you prepare your plan. The plan should be started several days before the assigned presentation, thus allowing you ample time for practicing the transposition, re-arranging the song (s), and thoroughly analyzing the music to be presented.

In planning for general music in the senior high school, you should follow the same pattern as shown in the elementary and junior high school. The class at this level usually includes both the pupil who needs an elective course for graduation and lacks proper motivation and the pupil who is sincerely interested in learning about music. The opportunity to challenge your students by providing a meaningful musical experience should be an exciting one. Even though they may

---

A UNIT FOR SECONDARY SCHOOL GENERAL MUSIC:
20TH CENTURY INNOVATIONS IN WRITING MUSIC

Objectives To acquaint pupils with the new music of the 20th century.
To acquaint the pupils with some of the composers involved in the new music.
To give pupils the opportunity to create their own music.

Materials Recordings of the music of:

Joseph Haydn	Edgar Varese
Wolfgang Mozart	Harry Partch
Henry Cowell	Arnold Schoenberg
John Cage	Anton Webern
Milton Babbitt	Alban Berg
Otto Luening	

Record player

Tape Recorder and tape

Various instruments: piano, tone blocks, gong, triangle, bongo drums, others as available

---

Activities Listen to the recordings
Discuss the writing techniques of each composer
Compare this music to that of, perhaps, Haydn or Mozart
Develop a vocabulary for discussion of contemporary music: electronic music, atonality, serial technique, microtone, aleatory, etc
Find sources of contemporary music sounds outside the classroom
Working in groups, experiment with making music, using instruments and objects at hand
Use tape recorder to record pupils' efforts at making their own music

---

Evaluation

Figure 5-4.

be less academically oriented than the advanced choir members, they may be stimulated into rewarding learning experiences by your careful planning.

The plan in Figure 5-4 provides an example of a suitable unit for either junior or senior high school general music. The length of time for the unit is determined by the pupils' interest.

This plan, like the fifth-grade unit, includes more material and activities than may be desired, However, it is wise to have extra material available for each lesson.

**A UNIT FOR SECONDARY SCHOOL GENERAL MUSIC:
THE MUSIC OF AARON COPLAND**

Objectives   To acquaint the pupils with the music and role in American music of a contemporary composer, Aaron Copland.

Materials   Record player
Recordings: *Rodeo*
            Billy the Kid
            Appalachian Spring
            Quiet City

Song: "Simple Gifts"

Film: *Appalachian Spring*

Activities   Pupils study the life and work of Copland, through reading, oral reports, and discussion.
Pupils evaluate Copland's importance in American music.
Pupils hear recordings of Copland's music.
Pupils see film of *Appalachian Spring.*
Pupils learn song.
Pupils collect pictures of Copland and illustrate music for bulletin boards.
Pupils attend ballet (*Rodeo, Billy the Kid, Appalachian Spring.*)

Evaluation

Figure 5-5.

Suitable for both junior and senior high school general music, the unit in Figure 5-5 is based upon listening experience. As in the previous plans, flexibility in choosing the music and the amount of time for the unit are provided. For example, in this unit you would surely choose to include *Appalachian Spring* and *Quiet City,* but would select either *Rodeo* or *Billy the Kid* rather than to attempt to use both compositions.

The flexibility as shown in the above plans is intended to emphasize for you again that there are many approaches to the organization of your lesson presentations. No specific order for the presentation of the unit material has been intended since this may vary from group to group. Also, as you plan with your pupils new directions to the unit may appear. If this occurs, be ready to adjust your planning and presentation.

Presentation

Having studied the factors involved in organization and having completed the lesson plan (s), you are now ready to begin the teaching phase. Although the lesson plan and the presentation are directly related, the superior written plan does not guarantee a successful presentation because of the unpredictable factor in the human beings who make up the class.

The following points apply to presentation at each grade level and should be considered before you present your first lesson:

1. Your basic objective in teaching the general music class is to guide your pupils' growth into intelligent, selective consumers of music.

2. The effectiveness of your teaching methods may be measured by the response of the pupils.

3. In the selection of presentation methods, consideration of the structure of the class schedule (daily, weekly, otherwise) should be given.

4. Your presentation should at all times involve your pupils in meaningful experiences in music.

5. You should avoid the teaching of facts outside a musical context.

At all levels and whatever the teaching method, you should prepare a lesson thoroughly. If referral to written material on the chalkboard is to be made, this should be prepared before the beginning of the class. Piano, instruments, tape recorder, record player, and records should be in place and ready to be used. If a film or film strip is to be presented preview it and arrange for its availability, along with the projector. For a lesson in which the pupils may wish to engage in further research, you should have checked for reference material in the school and public library. In essence, advance preparation should be so extensive that you can give full attention to guidance of the pupils to their highest potential during the class sessions. You may have before you a lesson plan or cue cards and the necessary materials, but use them only for brief referrals since eye contact with the pupils is vital. The importance of your mastery of the material may be shown in presenting, for instance, the story of an opera. The reading of a synopsis to a group of elementary or junior high school pupils is absolutely useless. However, if you tell the story in an exciting, interested manner, the pupils will be totally engrossed in your presentation. Another aid to an effective presentation is making use of your own particular talent and experiences—the ability to play an instrument or instruments, sharing mementos and remembered experiences of your travel, and other unusal experiences are positive assets in teaching.

As your teaching skill grows try what is commonly called teacher-pupil planning. More work and planning by the teacher are necessary than in the lecture method. Having decided on the basic topic or subject, you may discuss with your pupils the implementation of the learning. Your pupils' special contribution may be made by art projects, oral reports, research studies, recordings, musical presentations—all according to their special interest and ability. The length of time given to this type of plan depends upon your ability to lead the pupils, the class schedule, the developmental level of the pupils, and the type of unit to be developed. In the same manner, you should endeavor to increase your skill in guided questioning. In most instances, you should tell your pupils only enough to arouse their interest in individual or group research. Consistently telling the pupils every fact soon destroys their interest and initiative. In using the questioning procedure, try to develop skill in accepting and finding value in all answers given by pupils, whether correct or not. When you reject a pupil's answer because it is not the one you expect, you may close a door of communication and thereby lose your opportunity to interest the pupil in music.

Another important factor in effective teaching is pacing your lesson. Your lesson plan, as written, may show evidence of the content necessary for an effective lesson. However, the plan's success depends upon making it come alive as you teach. This, in turn, depends upon sensitivity to your pupils and the situation. The tempo of your speech pattern, diction, posture, the manner in which you move from one activity to another—all of these affect the pacing of your lesson.

In summary, teaching the general music class offers what may be the greatest challenge of all music teaching. Working without the glamor of the performance goals of the choir, you must depend upon your creative ability to meet the musical needs of all pupils and to increase their cultural education and sensitivity.

Elementary School Presentation

In the elementary school, the presentation phase of teaching actually begins as the children enter the room, or in the case of the "traveling" music teacher, when he enters. Your attitude will contribute to the children's eagerness and receptivity as they anticipate the day's activities. If planning has been thorough and if you feel secure in the lesson you have planned, you impart that security to your pupils. If you are frantically thumbing through a book searching for a particular song, the children, perhaps even subconsciously, lose some of their confidence and zest. Children can instantly discern the difference between the teacher who starts the period as though every minute is so precious it should not be wasted and the teacher who takes as much time as possible in calling the roll, thereby seeming to avoid actual contact with teaching.

As has been previously suggested, you may well begin the teaching phase with one class. As soon as you have experienced success add other classes until you are teaching all classes allowed by your cooperating teacher. In your early teaching your cooperating teacher will remain in the room. He will note suggestions for improvement and discuss these with you as quickly as possible. Build upon your strength and immediately seek to correct your errors. Although the college supervisor will be with you less consistently than the cooperating teacher, his visits will be followed by conferences in which your performance in the classroom will be discussed. Because habits are quickly formed, the observation and suggestions by your cooperating teacher and college supervisor are of great value to success in the teaching profession; they can help to establish superior teaching techniques. Also, both a tape recorder and video tape should be used during your classes so that you may later study and evaluate your performance as a teacher.

When you have successfully completed the early teaching phase the cooperating teacher will leave the room, at first for short periods of time, gradually lengthening these until you have the experience of being in complete charge. Ability to use the suggestions of your cooperating teacher and college supervisor should give you confidence and pleasure in teaching.

Secondary School Presentation

The beginning of the class in the junior and senior high school is of as great importance as in the elementary school. Pupils of these levels are capable of identifying their teachers' abilities more quickly than young children. Many have grown accustomed to boredom in school, in fact, may even appear to enjoy it. Your challenge is to "sell" your lesson to them—to make music alive and exciting. The idealism in this attitude is apparent, but it is not an impossible dream—many superior teachers daily accept the challenge. If you are absorbed in paper work and fail to acknowledge your pupils' entrance into the classroom, if you allow the pupils to mull about the room long after the appointed time for class, if you appear to be indifferent to them, no amount of pre-planning will make your presentation effective.

As in the elementary school, you may at first be assigned to one class, gradually adding others as your skill increases. Since the class period is usually longer than in the lower school, the cooperating teacher may give you a project for only a part of the time until you are ready to assume responsibility for the entire class period. Here, too, he may stay in the room, following the same procedure as in the elementary school. If he enters verbally into your presentation you should accept this as a cooperative effort, not a denial of your ability. The spirit of working together should serve to enhance, not to embarass you and your presentation.

Observe the same procedures as suggested in the elementary presentation discussion. Since there are various levels of maturity among junior and senior high school pupils generalization is difficult. As their school attendance has lengthened in years, so have the pupils' experience and interests tended to become more varied. Therefore, your vocabulary and approach must be attuned to this variance.

Evaluation

You will probably have more opportunity for objective evaluation of your pupils' growth in the general music area than in the choir program because of the differences in content and goals. However, be aware that a well written test on memorized facts does not necessarily indicate a high degree of musical growth. In order to increase your skill and develop as many teaching techniques as possible while you have the opportunity to work with the college supervisor and the cooperating teacher, you should analyze your progress, using their suggestions for improvement. Along with the observations of your own teaching via tape recorder and video tape, observation of other teachers, experienced and novice, will be of particular value to you at this point.

As guidelines for your self-evaluation, the following suggestions are given:

1. Are my lesson plans flexible?
2. Is there sufficient variety in the activities of my classes?
3. Are my pupils interested, bored, excited, or tired in my classes?
4. Are all phases of the general music program represented, or does one area, such as listening, dominate my classes?
5. Are objectives for the classes clearly focused?
6. Is the learning situation so structured that every pupil participates?
7. If some pupils fail to participate in the class, what techniques do I use to arouse their interest?
8. Is there tangible evidence of continuous musical growth in my pupils?
9. Is my teaching based on the memorization of facts?
10. Is my teaching based on my pupils' understanding of broad concepts?
11. Is there evidence of my pupils' increasing interest in music?
12. Is the quality of music used of worthwhile importance? Is it challenging?

As in all phases of teaching, evaluation is on-going, continuous, and necessary for growth of both teacher and pupils. Interest in the acceptance of the evaluation of your supervisors serves as an indication of your probable success and satisfaction in the teaching career.

Suggestions For Further Reading

Andrews, Frances M., and Joseph A. Leeder, Guiding Junior High School Pupils in Music Experiences. *Englewood Cliffs, N.J.: Prentice-Hall, Inc., 1963, Chapters 3, 4, and 6.*

Cheyette, Irving, and Herbert Cheyette, Teaching Music Creatively in the Elementary School. *New York: McGraw-Hill Company, 1969.*

Dello Joio, Norman, et al, "The Contemporary Music Project for Creativity in Music Education," Music Educators Journal, *LIV, No. 7 (1968), 41-72.*

Ernst, Karl D., and Charles L. Gary, Music in General Education. *Music Educators National Conference, 1965.*

———, The Study of Music in the Elementary School: A Conceptual Approach. *Music Educators National Conference, 1967.*

Hipple, Walter J., Jr. "Humanities in the Secondary Schools," Music Educators Journal, *LIV, No. 6 (1968), 85-88, 155-161.*

Maslow, Abraham H., "Music Education and Peak Experience," Music Educators Journal, *LIV, No. 6 (1968), 73-75, 163-171.*

Monsour, Sally, Marilyn Cohen, and Patricia Lindell, Rhythms in Music and Dance for Children. *Belmont, California: Wadsworth Publishing Co., 1966, Part III.*

Nash, Grace C., Music with Children, *Series I, II, III, Chicago, Ill.: Kitching Educational Division of Ludwig Industries, 1969.*

Olson, Rees G., "Teaching Music Concepts by the Discovery Method," Music Educators Journal, *LIV, No. 1 (1967), 51-53, 123-131.*

Orff, Carl, and Gunild Keetman, Music for Children. *New York: Schott Music Corp. (Associated Music Publishers, Inc.), 1960.*

Price, Gertrude, "Improvisation in the Elementary Classroom," Music Educators Journal, *LIV, No. 8 (1968), 42-47.*

Reimer, Bennett, "Curriculum Reforms and the Junior High General Music Class," Music Educators Journal, *LIII, No. 2 (1966), 42-44, 123-127.*

———, "Performance and Aesthetic Sensitivity," *Music Educators Journal (1968), 27-29, 107-114.*

Russell-Smith, Geoffrey, "Introducing Kodaly Principles into Elementary Teaching," Music Educators Journal, *LIV, No. 3 (1967), 43-45.*

Sur, William R., and Charles F. Schuller, Music Education for Teen-Agers. *New York: Harper & Row, Publishers, 1966, Chapters 2, 3, 4, 7, and 10.*

6

The Organization
and Development
of the Performing Group

The student teaching program provides an opportunity for you to study the techniques used by your cooperating teacher as he develops the orchestra, band, or choir. Although you may not be directly involved in some of the facets of organization, develop an awareness of effective organizational techniques. Since performance is one of the main functions of a musical organization, especially in the secondary school, the director is responsible for everything pertaining to performance. This means that in addition to the musical aspects of the performance the director must have a knowledge of lighting, staging, programming, drama, and stage presence. It is also the responsibility of the director to see that people know about the program so that they will attend the performance. The director will be responsible for all news releases and other forms of publicity.

Since a musical organization is actively engaged in a variety of performances, it is possible that the school system can afford to finance only a portion of the items needed by the group. Uniforms, tours, awards, instruments, and music may call for additional funds which may have to be raised by the director, his students, and patrons. To help finance the organization it may be necessary for the director to organize and work with a parent organization.

One of the primary aspects of the job of music director is the attraction and retention of students. Since instrumental and choral organizations are generally offered on an elective basis, it will be the responsibility of the director to sell himself and his program to the student body.

As a student teacher, you will need to be aware of techniques of recruitment of students, the development of patron organizations, the formulation of budgets and methods of fund raising, the selection and maintenance of uniforms, the sources of publicity, and the development of award programs. The following chapter will guide you as you work with your cooperating teacher in these areas.

Recruitment of Students

If you have the priviledge of working with a well balanced performing organization in your student teaching assignment, you should begin to wonder how your cooperating teacher managed to have the proper instrumentation or voices in the group. If only a few students participate in the organization, you should be curious concerning the reason. In either case, musical organizations do not just happen. Behind each group—large or small, balanced or deficient—you will find a recruitment philosophy and plan. As in any other endeavor, some recruitment programs are well organized and highly successful while others are less than adequate. A thorough understanding of recruitment theories and techniques will be needed before you assume the position of an orchestra, band or choir director.

Developing a Theory of Recruitment

The open end questionnaire-interview research technique should provide interesting and informative answers to recruitment questions. With the approval of your cooperating teacher, ask the members of each performing organization to fill out the form shown in Figure 6-1.

This form may be adapted for band and choral students. In cases where the answers given by the students are unclear, you may find it necessary to follow

---

MUSIC QUESTIONNAIRE—STRING STUDENTS

1. What grade are you in at your school? _____

2. What string instrument do you play in orchestra? _____

3. Do you study privately? _____

   If so, with whom do you study? _____
4. What grade were you in when you first enrolled in orchestra as a beginning string

   student? _____

5. When you were a beginner, why did you choose to play a string instrument?

   _____

6. Do other members of your family play an instrument? If so, which members and

   what instruments do they play? _____

   _____

Figure 6-1.

INSTRUMENTAL QUESTIONNAIRE DATA			
Reasons given for membership in organization	*Times given*	*Reasons for selection of instrument*	*Times given*

Figure 6-2.

the questionnaires with interviews, thereby providing a better understanding of the motives underlying organizational membership.

After the data has been received, a list showing the reasons given for membership and the frequency of occurrence should be compiled. A form similar to that shown in Figure 6-2 would be suitable for the tabulation of information.

This form may be adapted as needed by choir directors. Reasons for membership should provide a key to the development of the recruitment program in your community. As a student teacher, examine the following points concerning the recruitment of students:

1. Needs of the Organization

How does a director plan his program so that he has a balance of instrumentation or voices?

2. Physical Characteristics of the Students

What physical characteristics are most advantageous for performers on various instruments? How does the instrumental director convince a student that he might be more comfortable on one of the other string instruments if he is too small for string bass? How does the choral director keep pace with the changing voices of the adolescent singers?

3. Musical Aptitude

Is so-called "musical aptitude" to be considered in the selection and placement of students? What are the advantages and disadvantages in the use of musical aptitude tests for the purposes of recruitment? What tests are available in this area?

4. Grade Level of the Student

Is the recruitment program in the elementary school basically different from that of the junior and senior high school?

5. Mental-Emotional Factors

In instrumental music, is the slow learner assigned to the same type of instrument as the rapid, alert thinker? Are instruments such as oboe given to special types of students? Is the moving of "slower" students from violin to viola educationally valid?

The cooperating teacher may consider factors other than those listed above. You should be aware of his philosophy and study various recruitment plans.

Recruitment Techniques

In developing recruitment techniques, it will be found that the situation usually dictates the methods used in attracting students to the music class or the performing organization.

Two types of students are available to the music director. First, there is the student who has previously participated in the orchestra, band, or choir but did not enroll in the current school organization. He may actually play or sing relatively well and may only need a few words of encouragement from the director. The music survey provides one means of discovering students who have played an instrument or have sung in a choir. The survey forms (Figure 6-3 and Figure 6-4) are suggestive of the types that might be used in the school.

In administering the music survey, it is often wise to have the form distributed by each homeroom teacher, filled out during the homeroom period, and returned to the homeroom teacher at the end of the time allotted for the completion of the form. The music director studies each form and talks with the homeroom teacher before arranging conferences with prospective students and parents.

The second type of student available to the director is the beginner. The techniques used in attracting the students to the music program are varied. In all probability your cooperating teacher uses a combination of the following recruitment techniques:

INSTRUMENTAL MUSIC SURVEY

Name _____ Homeroom _____ Grade _____

Address_____ Telephone _____ School _____

Parents' names_____

Parents' occupations _____

Please check the following musical instruments that you have played or now play:

piano	flute	trumpet
violin	piccolo	french horn
viola	oboe	trombone
cello	clarinet	baritone
bass	bassoon	tuba
percussion	saxophone	other inst.

How long have you played the above instrument? _____

Do you own the instrument checked? _____

What orchestra, band, or choir experience have you had?

_____

_____

Check if you are now enrolled in the school orchestra _____,

band _____ , or choir _____ .

On the reverse side of this form, please list your complete class schedule—name of class, teacher, time, room number.

Figure 6-3.

1. Newspaper Articles

Stories are published in the local newspapers telling of the formation of new music classes and membership opportunities in performing organizations.

2. Posters

Posters, telling of the organization, are placed in the school and community.

3. Patron Organizations

Members of the patron organization assist in the dissemination of information

---

CHORAL SURVEY

Name _____ Homeroom _____ Grade_____

Address_____ Telephone _____ School _____

Parents' names_____

Parents' occupations _____

Have you ever sung in a choir? _____ If so, where? _____

What vocal part have you sung? _____

Check if you are now enrolled in the school orchestra _____, band_____,

or choir_____ .
On the reverse side of this form, please list your complete class schedule—name of
class, teacher, time, room number.

Figure 6-4.

concerning the advantages of membership in the organization by talking with other parents. Often letters explaining the opportunities available in music are sent to the parents of prospective students.

4. *Current Students*

Members of the performing organization interest their friends in the performing group by personal communication.

5. *Counselors and Faculty Members*

Counselors and members of the faculty tell students about the music program. They are in a position to guide students toward music and may do so if they consider the music department to be of significant value in the educational process.

6. *Demonstration Concerts*

Prospective students are given the opportunity to hear other students through demonstration concerts. For instance, prospective string students may be invited to play rhythms pizzicato on the open strings while the teacher or the members of the organization play the melody and harmony parts of a folk song.

Prospective choir students may be invited to sing with the school choir in an exploratory program. There are numerous varieties of the demonstration concert ranging from a solo performance to a concert presented by a one-hundred piece band.

Because of the dropout rate between elementary and secondary school, the junior high school director frequently works out a plan whereby he can be associated with the students in the elementary school before they come to the junior high school. For example, the junior high school director may give a spring concert and invite all sixth graders from his feeder schools to participate. This gives the elementary school student an opportunity to know both the director and the junior high school students in a performance setting. A similar type of performance is suitable in moving from junior to senior high school.

During the student teaching term it would be well for you to list your own ideas as well as those of your cooperating teacher, so that you may later call upon a reserve of information concerning the recruitment of students.

Patron Organizations

The patron organization for a band, orchestra or choir consists, for the most part, of the parents of the students. Occasionally, parents of former students and interested citizens participate in the organization's activities. Patron organizations can be formed at each level—elementary and secondary—as the situation requires.

As a rule, these organizations should be organized only when there is a definite need and should be for service rather than social activities. Since the patron organization is optional, you may or may not find this type of group at your assignment. However, be aware of its role and methods of organization.

The purposes of the patron organization may be to assist in fund raising, to provide transportation, to sponsor programs, and to assist in the recruitment of new students. The success of the group as a service organization depends chiefly upon the leadership of the director in providing specific goals.

One very important aspect of the patron organization is that of providing reinforcement of the learning situation. Parents of younger children are often encouraged to attend classes and are shown ways whereby they can intelligently assist the child as he practices at home. At the secondary level the parents are sometimes guided by the music director so that they may better understand the educational goals of the organization. In each instance the parents are shown techniques for helping their children as they develop musically.

The following committees are typical of those included in the organization of the group:

Program committee: The purpose of the program committee is that of booking the organization for performances in the community.

Uniform committee: The purposes of the uniform committee are to assist in the selection, purchase, and maintenance of uniforms for the organization.

Publicity committee: The purpose of this committee is that of notifying the public of all programs to be presented by the organization in the school and the community.

Transportation committee: The purpose of the transportation committee is to arrange for the transportation of orchestra, band, or choir members and guest clinicians.

Budget committee: The purpose of the budget committee is to assist in providing means for the financing of the activities of the organization.

At the high school level the duties of some of these committees may be assumed by student members of the organization. The choice of whether or not to have a patron organization is usually the decision of the director. You should consider the following questions in studying the role of your cooperating teacher as he works with the patron organization:

1. How was the group organized?
2. What are the offices of the organization?
3. What are the purposes of the organization?
4. What committees exist? How are the members of the committees selected? Is the committee chairman appointed by the director or elected by the members of the committee?
5. When does the organization meet? How often are general meetings held? Does the music director attend all meetings? Where does the group meet?
6. What are the educational purposes of the organization?

Budget and Fund Raising

Although a budget is usually provided for music and instruments, such items as tape recorders, a stereo phonograph, uniforms, office supplies, tours and trips, printed programs, tickets, pictures, posters, scholarship funds, and awards may not be included. As a prospective music director, you should be aware of the possibility that additional funds may be needed.

Budget

Prior to planning a long range budget, the director must take inventory of his

INVENTORY		
Item	*Cost of Item*	*Source of Funds*

Figure 6-5.

present equipment. You may receive valuable training during your student teaching term by using the chart shown in Figure 6-5 in determining the equipment status of the organization at your assignment.

Among those items to be considered in planning a budget for the musical organization are:

1. Music library:
   a. Music
   b. Manuscript paper
   c. Periodicals
   d. Books
   e. Films

2. Instruments:
   a. Purchase
   b. Repair fund

3. Equipment:
   a. Tape recorder
   b. Tapes
   c. Phonograph
   d. Records
   e. Tuning device
   f. Music stands: stationary and folding
   g. Air conditioning
   h. Instrument storage racks
   i. Music storage racks
   j. Special chairs: string bass and tuba
   k. Risers
   l. Shells for stages and outdoor performances
   m. Television sets for ETV
   n. Overhead projector

    o. Conductor's chair
    p. Conductor's podium

4. Uniforms:
    a. Purchase
    b. Maintenance

5. Office supplies:
    a. Stationery
    b. Envelopes
    c. Stencils and carbons
    d. Miscellaneous items

6. Tours and trips:
    a. Performances in city
    b. Out of town trips
    c. Clinics and festivals

7. Publicity:
    a. Posters
    b. Pictures of organization
    c. Printed programs
    d. Tickets for programs
    e. Newsletters

8. Awards:
    a. Standard and special awards
    b. Scholarships

It is the director's responsibility to make sure that his organization has necessary equipment. Frequently, an organization is deprived of equipment simply because the director failed to ask for the item.

Fund Raising

Before formulating fund raising plans, the director should acquaint himself with school policy. A desirable method in one community might be detrimental to the program in another setting. The following fund raising methods have been used in various communities throughout the United States:

a. Concerts

b. Candy sales

c. Dances

d. Auctions

e. Bridge, bingo parties

f. Bake sales

g. Tag sales: "I AM AN ORCHESTRA BOOSTER"

h. Renting instruments to students

i. Sale of records

j. Halloween carnivals

k. Uniform rental fees

l. Mowing lawns

m. Car washes

n. Paper drives

o. Baby sitting

p. Christmas card sales

q. Suppers

r. Donations: clubs and individuals

Some of the above methods consume excessive time while producing limited financial results. The director will need to consider not only the amount of profit involved in the activity but also the demand for the service or item in the community. Frequently, other organizations in the school are engaged in fund raising projects. It is best not to sell identical services or products. Also, it is generally more desirable to conduct one or two major fund raising projects rather than to have several small drives. The following questions should be raised in talking with your cooperating teacher concerning fund raising:

1. What fund raising plans are used by the organization?

2. When do fund raising drives take place?

3. How much money is usually raised by each plan?

4. Who works in the fund raising program?

5. What is the financial goal for the year?

6. How are the funds used?

Uniforms

Each musical group—orchestra, band, and choir—should have some type of performance uniform. As a future director, you must be aware of the factors involved in the selection, purchase, and maintenance of uniforms.

Selecting the Uniform

The choice of the uniform for the organization will depend upon a combination of the following factors:

1. The Cultural Expectations of the School and the Community

The appropriateness of the style of the uniform will vary according to the school and the community. The students must feel that the uniform is suitable for them and they must be proud to be seen in the apparel.

2. The Age of the Members of the Organization

A uniform becoming to a high school student may not be appropriate for a junior high school student. The age of the student must be considered in selecting the uniform.

3. Type of Presentations Given by the Organization

The time of day, the setting for the program, and the type of music influence the choice of a uniform. For instance, the choir presenting a program of sacred music in the morning appears best in robes. The same choir in a concert of secular music should use another type of dress.

Frequently, a uniform is selected for its versatility. For example, band uniforms may be worn with an overlay for marching and without for concert performances. A change in the style of tie will either dress up or dress down a uniform.

4. The Uniform Budget

Finances must be considered prior to the selection of uniforms. The director should determine the number of uniforms needed and the amount of funds available before the uniform selection committee is formed.

Manufacture of the Uniform

Uniforms may be obtained from the following sources:

1. A professional seamstress.
2. Parents.
3. Local clothing stores.
4. Professional uniform manufacturers.

The following professional uniform manufacturers are among those available to the director:

Bentley and Simon, Inc., 7th W. 36th St., New York, N. Y.

De Moulin Brothers & Co., Greenville, Ill.

E. R. Moore Co., 932 Dakin St., Chicago, Ill.

Thomas A. Peterson Co., 601 E. 33rd St., Kansas City, Mo.

Rollins Blazers, Inc., 242 Park Ave. So., New York, N. Y.

Saxony Clothes, 198 Canal St. (Dept. MEJ) New York, N. Y.

Uniforms by Ostwald, Inc., Ostwald Bldg., Staten Island, N.Y.

C. E. Ward Co., New London, Ohio.

Financing the Uniforms

The financing of the uniforms may come from a combination of these sources:

1. School activity fund.
2. Funds raised by orchestra, band, or choir members.
3. Contributions from interested individuals and civic organizations.
4. Funds raised by the patron organization.
5. Uniform rental fees.

Maintenance of Uniforms

The school usually assumes the responsibility for furnishing extra uniforms and for replacing worn garments. Members of the organization generally pay for the cleaning of the uniforms at the end of the year. In some instances a nominal fee is charged for the rental of the uniforms, thereby providing funds for maintenance and replacement. Since there is an economic advantage in quantity buying, extra uniforms should be purchased with the initial selection.

To summarize, you should be aware of the factors involved in the selection, purchase, and maintenance of uniforms for the musical organization. The following questions should be directed to your cooperating teacher so that you may better understand the uniform system used at your school:

1. When were the present uniforms purchased?
2. How were the style of the uniform and the manufacturer selected? Who was responsible for making the selection?
3. How much did the uniforms cost? How were they financed?
4. How are the uniforms marked for identification?
5. What plan is used in issuing the uniforms?

6. Is there a uniform fee? If so, who collects this? Where is the money kept? For what purpose is the money used?

7. How many extra uniforms were purchased? What sizes were included? Are the sizes of the uniforms such that they are representative of the average group so that a change in student members does not create a serious uniform problem? Are a few uniforms of atypical sizes (large and small) included? If so, what is the range of the sizes of the uniform?

8. How are the uniforms maintained? How often are extra uniforms purchased? Who pays for the cleaning of the uniforms? How often are the uniforms cleaned? Where are the uniforms stored?

Publicity

During the student teaching period, you should have an opportunity to assist your cooperating teacher with news releases and other phases of the public information program.

The cooperating teacher may ask you to write an article for the local or school newspaper. After the article is written the cooperating teacher should edit the work. Although the task of reporting the news may be assigned to a student or parent, the director is always responsible for news releases concerning his organization.

Purposes of Publicity

Publicity must be carefully planned if it is to assist in the development and promotion of the music department. Oral and written reports of the activities of the musical organization are usually made available to the public for one of the following reasons:

1. To Inform the Public

News items are released for the purpose of advertising a concert, informing the public of the organization of music classes or groups, or announcing special awards and honors earned by the organization and its members.

2. To Modify Public Opinions

Items are written for the purpose of modifying the opinions of a segment of the public. For example, the orchestra director may find that his organization is limited to one or two performance opportunities per semester. In this case, he may develop a series of news releases displaying the potential versatility of the orchestra in an attempt to change the image of the organization in the school and the community.

Sources for Publicity

The placing of news releases will vary according to the size of the community and the facilities within the school. The following outlets are usually available to the director of the organization:

1. Newspapers

School and community newspapers are the primary source in the distribution of information concerning the musical organization. The following basic rules should be observed in writing all news articles:

1. Type and double-space each article.
2. The first paragraph should contain five ingredients—who, when, what, where, and why.
3. Space should be left at the top of the article so that the editor of the paper may insert a caption.
4. The upper right-hand corner should have the name and address of the writer and the suggested date of publication.
5. Glossy prints of pictures should be used for best reproduction.

The use of pictures with news articles is very effective. To present a favorable impression, the organization should be presented in a professional manner. Every boy should wear dark socks, the same type tie, and the same color coat. Girls should avoid drawing attention to themselves by wearing jewelry unless the item is a part of the uniform.

2. Public Address System Announcements

Announcements are usually made daily over the school's public address system. The music director can use these for the purpose of informing the student body of the activities of the organization. For example, the following announcement depicts an orchestra in a favorable manner:

The bus taking the orchestra to the Civic auditorium will leave from the school parking lot tomorrow morning at 7:30. Orchestra members are to be excused from their first period classes at 9:00. The orchestra will present a concert at 11:30 and will perform tomorrow evening at 7:30 in a massed group with other high school orchestras.

This type of announcement gives needed information to the members of the organization and provides publicity in an attractive manner.

3. Posters

The announcement of a music program may be enhanced by the use of descriptive posters. A story may be told effectively in a minimum amount of time with very little effort on the part of the viewer through the visual assistance of posters. Members of the organization should be given the opportunity to design and create appropriate posters to be displayed throughout the school and the community.

4. Other Mediums

In addition to the previously cited sources of publicity, the director may find that it is possible to direct news through the mediums of radio, television, local business firms, civic organizations, and parents. Each communication source should be explored by the director and remembered as a potential publicity aid.

The following questions concerning publicity should be discussed with your cooperating teacher:

1. What publicity sources are available in the school and the community? Of these sources, which ones are used by your cooperating teacher?

2. When are news releases issued? What is the purpose of the release? Are pictures included in the release?

3. Who compiles the material for the news releases?

Awards

The primary purpose of an awards program is to allow the director an opportunity to recognize those students who have made significant musical growth and have given outstanding service to the organization throughout the year. Be aware of the factors involved in organizing and administering an awards program for a musical organization.

Types of Awards

A standard award for each successive year of service in the musical organization is frequently given. These awards are earned by individuals who meet the specific requirements set forth at the beginning of the school year. For example, in the three year secondary school, the following items might be used as standard awards:

> First year   Felt letter
> Second year   Merit pin or key
> Third year   Trophy

In addition to the standard award, special awards are often presented to:

1. The outstanding musician.
2. The outstanding ensembles.
3. The students giving superior service to the organization.

Criteria for Awards

The following factors are among those usually considered in determining a student's eligibility for receiving an award:

1. Performances with the organization.
2. Extra rehearsals attended.
3. Individual improvement in musicianship.
4. Participation in solo-ensemble programs.
5. Attitude.
6. Service to the organization.
7. Concert attendance as a listener.

Many directors use a point system to evaluate the students. In this plan, the students are allotted a certain number of points for each of the criteria items. Members of the organization frequently work with the director in the development of a point system. A pre-determined number of points is usually required before the student is considered eligible for an award at the end of the year.

Presentation of Awards

Awards are frequently presented at the spring concert, the school awards assembly, or the fine arts department banquet.

The setting for the presentation of the awards should enhance the value of the program. Frequently, the music director invites the principal or the music supervisor to participate in the presentation of the awards.

It is possible that you may have an opportunity to view an awards program duri⌐g your tenure as a student teacher. The following questions may be used in studying awards programs:

1. What is the purpose of the awards program?
2. What types of awards are given to the members of the organization?
3. Where are the awards purchased? What is the cost of each award? How is the awards program financed?
4. How are recipients of awards selected?
5. When and where are awards presented? Who presents the awards to the students?

Suggestions For Further Reading

Decker, Harold A., *"Choosing Music for Performance,"* Choral Director's Guide, *Kenneth L. Neidig and John W. Jennings. West Nyack, N.Y.: Parker Publishing Co., Inc. 1967, Chapter 5.*

Diercks, Louis, *"Public Relations,"* Choral Director's Guide, eds. *Kenneth L. Neidig and John W. Jennings. West Nyack, N.Y.: Parker Publishing Co., Inc., 1967, Chapter 2.*

Draper, Dallas, *"Contest and Festivals,"* Choral Director's Guide, eds. *Kenneth L. Neidig and John W. Jennings. West Nyack, N.Y.: Parker Publishing Co., Inc., 1967, Chapter 7.*

Duvall, W. Clyde, The High School Bank Director's Handbook. *Englewood Cliffs, N.J.: Prentice-Hall, Inc., 1960.*

Edwards, William, *"The Recruitment of Beginners,"* The Instrumentalist, *XXIII, No. 2 (1968), 48-49.*

Gaines, Joan, Approaches to Public Relations for the Music Educator. *Washington, D.C.: Music Educators National Conference, 1968.*

Garretson, Robert L., Conducting Choral Music. *Allyn & Bacon, Inc., 1963, Chapters 5 and 6.*

Graham, Floyd Freeman, Public Relations in Music Education. *New York: Exposition Press, 1954.*

Ivy, James, *"Come Blow Your Horn-An Invitation,"* The Instrumentalist, *XXIII, No. 2 (1968), 49-50.*

Lehman, Paul R., Tests and Measurements in Music. *Englewood Cliffs, N.J.: Prentice-Hall, Inc., 1968.*

Orchestra Planning Guide, *National School Orchestra Association, High School, Benton Harbor, Michigan, 1962.*

Sur, William R., and Charles F. Schuller, Music Education for Teen-Agers. *New York: Harper & Row Publishers, 1966. Chapters 9 and 13.*

7

Obtaining a Teaching Position

Since obtaining a teaching position may require extended time, it is important to begin the process from six to ten weeks before your college graduation date. At the same time, have an application photograph made. In seeking a position, several avenues of approach are open to you:

1. The placement office in your college.
2. Direct application to school districts of your choice.
3. Professional placement agencies.
4. Personal contacts among friends and acquaintances.

You may avail yourself of one or more of these avenues simultaneously. However, you are bound to work through the agency which first informs you of a position. Seek the advice of your college supervisor in deciding the best procedure for your individual needs.

Your college placement office, if active, offers you some decided advantages:

1. It is near you.
2. Colleges have a special interest in placing their graduates in satisfactory positions.
3. Your personal record file is kept in an organized manner so that you may use it for future positions.
4. You will not be required to pay a percentage of your first year's salary, as is necessary with the professional placement agency.

Even though you may not plan to teach immediately after college graduation, you should register with this office. One important reason is that references from the members of the college faculty and your cooperating teacher(s) should be compiled at this time so that these persons may easily recall the quality of

---

March 15, 1971

Personnel Director
Middletown Independent School District
Middletown, Kansas

Dear Sir:

I am interested in obtaining a position as band director in the Middletown School District for the next school year, beginning in September, 1971. I would appreciate your sending an application form to me so that I may file my credentials with you. Should a vacancy occur in your system, I would greatly appreciate being considered for the position.

Very truly yours,

John Jones

John Jones
000 Main Street
Northtown, North Dakota

Figure 7-1.

your class work and your student teaching. The registration fee charged by the college placement office is usually very nominal and in terms of your future teaching positions, inconsequential.

If you wish to teach in a particular school district, you may apply directly to the director of personnel in that district. Your initial contact should be a letter indicating your desire to teach in the district and your request for an application for a teaching position. You should enclose a stamped self-addressed envelope. This letter need not contain other information since the personnel director considers your qualifications only as shown on the district's application and through the recommendations of your references as filed on the specific forms used by the district. Figure 7-1 is an example of a suitable letter.

The professional placement agency usually charges a nominal service fee for registration, but you must also sign an agreement that you will pay the agency a percentage of your first year's salary for the position obtained through the agency's service. Upon completion of the registration procedure, you will receive notices of available positions. You may choose to contact only those that are of interest to you. An advantage of registration with this type of placement office is that you may learn of positions in all parts of the United States rather than in only the more limited territory served by your college office.

In seeking a position through personal contacts your association with your college faculty and other school personnel may help you to procure a teaching position. It is important that you let your professional friends know that you are seeking a position. Although suitable positions are often obtained through this medium, it is less organized and to a certain extent less certain than the other avenues suggested above. Used as an adjunct to the others, it may be fruitful.

Regardless of the method used in obtaining a position some factors are of great importance. How you handle these may have positive influence on your success. Some guidelines for your assistance will be suggested in the ensuing discussion.

Applications

Although the desired information concerning the prospective teacher is basically the same for all school systems, the application form may vary from city to city. Consequently, you should study the entire application before beginning to complete it, thereby avoiding duplicate answers, redundancy, and errors. Unless otherwise specified, typing is preferred. Make direct, concise answers to questions. If any answer demands an answer of more than one sentence, you should compose the answer on another paper, copying it on the application, thereby avoiding erasures which mar the neat appearance of the completed form.

The photograph which is usually requested should show a pleasant expression, conservative attire, and attractive hair style. It should be stapled or clipped to the application. Your name should be signed on the back of the photograph. A transcript of the college record of your courses and grades should also be attached to the application by a clip.

Figure 7-2 is an example of those used by public schools.

The recommendations of those people who best know your capabilities are very important to you. Before including names or references you should ask each person if you may include him as a reference. In listing references on the application form, be certain to spell names correctly and to give exact addresses. Each reference listed will receive a form similar to Figure 7-3 whereby he will give his confidential opinion of your abilities.

After you have obtained a position, you should write a letter of appreciation to each reference and tell him about your new job.

Interviews

After studying your application and recommendations to ascertain suitability for the desired position, the personnel director may invite you to a personal

RETURN TO OFFICE OF
SUPERINTENDENT
202 WEST COLLEGE

GRAND PRAIRIE PUBLIC SCHOOLS
GRAND PRAIRIE, TEXAS

APPLICATION
(Do Not Use Typewriter)

PLEASE ATTACH
PHOTOGRAPH

All Employees Are Required To Live in Grand Prairie

Date _____

| Name | Present Address | Telephone | Permanent Address | Telephone |

EDUCATION

NAME OF SCHOOL AND LOCATION Include High School, College, Graduate Work and Summer Sessions in Order Taken	DATES	Hours Semester Credits	Kind of Degree	MAJOR SUBJECT And Semester Hours Credit	FIRST MINOR SUBJECT And Semester Hours Credit	LIST COLLEGE ACTIVITIES ENGAGED IN	SUBJECTS WHICH APPLICANT DESIRES TO TEACH In Order of Preference Specify—H.S., Junior H.S. or Grades

EXPERIENCE (List Recent Experience First)

NAME OF SCHOOL AND LOCATION	DATE	Number of Months	No. of Teachers in System	NATURE OF WORK If Grades, Specify What Grades and Subjects; if High School, the Subjects Taught and the Extra Curricular Work Handled	NAME OF SUPERINTENDENT AND PRESENT ADDRESS IF KNOWN

State your philosophy of education in not less than seventy-five words.

_____

_____

_____

_____

_____

_____

College hours elementary education _____   College hours secondary education _____

Figure 7-2.

PERSONAL DATA

Name in Full _____ Age _____ Height _____ Weight _____ Native State or Country? _____

Condition of Health for Past Two Years? _____ No. days lost last year because of illness? _____

Any Physical defects? _____ Is your hearing perfect? _____ Is your vision perfect? _____

Married? _____ No. of children? _____ Have you ever been married? _____ Husband's occupation? _____

What kind of certificate? _____ When granted? _____ Expiration? _____

Underscore those activities which you are able to direct or coach: Band, Choral Music, Student Council, Drama, Clubs, Debate, Declamation, Football, Baseball, Basketball, Track, Student Publications, List Others: _____

Do you sing? _____ List instruments you play? _____

Amount of last annual salary? _____ Total number years teaching experience: _____

If elected, and conditions prove satisfactory, do you plan to teach here at least two years? _____

When could you begin work? _____ Could you come for an interview? _____ Have you enclosed recent photograph? _____

Name at least two professional books which you have read during the past year. _____

What educational journals do you subscribe for? _____

What others do you read? _____

Have you been re-elected to your present position? _____ Church Preference _____

Can you teach public school music? _____ In what grades? _____

List teaching minors: (12 sem. hr. or more), if any, that are not shown elsewhere on this application: _____

This space for additional questions or remarks: _____

REFERENCES: These should be persons qualified to answer your fitness for the position you seek. Indicate any who are related to you.

NAME	ADDRESS	OCCUPATION

Figure 7-2 cont.

87

NORTHTOWN INDEPENDENT SCHOOL DISTRICT
000 Main St.
Northtown, North Dakota

REFERENCE BLANK

Mr. John Jones   has applied to the Northtown
Public Schools for a position to teach in the field of
instrumental music   . Will you please state your opinion of this
applicant's personal and professional qualifications as indicated by the items
below. This report is strictly confidential. Your cooperation is greatly
appreciated.

	Excellent	Good	Average	Poor
Personality				
Personal appearance				
General health				
Social qualities				
Emotional stability				
Professional loyalty and cooperation				
Adequacy of professional training				
Use of oral and written English				
Voice and speech				
Ability to organize and project teaching materials				
Understanding of pupils				
Evidence of professional growth				
Probable success as a teacher				

Would you employ the above as a teacher: Yes   No

In what professional capacity have you known the applicant? _____

For how long? _____

Remarks:

Name _____
Position _____
Date _____   Address _____

Figure 7-3.

interview. If possible, it is advisable to accept the suggested time; if you cannot arrange your schedule accordingly, you should immediately request another date. If the personnel director considers you an asset to the school district, he may arrange for you to meet with the school principal and the music supervisor in separate interviews.

Your preparation for the interview should include an unhurried, relaxed period before the actual meeting. Your self confidence may be bolstered by the realization that the invitation to the interview indicates genuine interest in your professional qualifications; otherwise, the busy personnel director would not take time for it. Likewise, if you have progressed to an interview with a principal and music supervisor, you obviously have the personnel director's support. In both cases, sufficient rest, ample time for travel to the interview, and correct attire enter into your imparting a favorable impression as you meet the administrator(s).

The interview provides the opportunity for mutual exploration of educational philosophies, goals, capabilities and attitudes. It involves "selling" and "buying". On the one side, the personnel director, principal, and music supervisor are describing the virtues of their program and are considering the value of your services to the school system. On the other hand, you are selling yourself and your ability and, at the same time, endeavoring to decide whether you wish to affiliate with this system. This is a time for careful listening, for practical thinking, for comprehensive questions, and for objective consideration of all factors. Since there is no standard interview approach or content, it is impossible to alert you to the exact questions you may be asked. Of course, you should allow the administrator(s) to set the climate of the interview and to begin the questions.

However, some information concerning the teaching position is vital to you as you make a decision to accept or reject a position. You will be expected to ask questions and may even be judged by the quality and quantity of your questions. Here are some guidelines to assist you in this important facet of the interview:

1. Prepare your questions before the interview.
2. Ask only pertinent questions.
3. State the questions concisely and directly.
4. Obtain information concerning: the philosophy and goals of the school system; the place of music in the curriculum at all levels; the time given to music at all levels; the number of class periods per day and the number of required courses; the salary schedule; increment and future salary goals; the fringe benefits, such as retirement, hospitalization, insurance, sick leave; the cultural benefits in the community; the socio-economic state of the community; the teachers' freedom in social life outside the school.

5. Maintain a courteous attitude during questions. Give thoughtful attention to the administrators' answers.

It is usually best to delay committing yourself to a definite acceptance or rejection of a position during the interview. The time for informing the personnel director of your decision should be decided at the close of the interview and may extend for twenty-four hours or more. This time will give you the opportunity to think objectively about the situation and to weigh the assets and liabilities. You will want to be absolutely certain of your decision before giving an affirmative answer or signing a contract, since it is unwise to refuse to honor an agreement made. In fact, after you have signed a contract you should fulfill it except in the case of a real emergency, since your professional reputation may be damaged if you fail to meet your commitment. Also, you should look forward to remaining in the teaching assignment a minimum of two or three years. A record of several one year positions is, to say the least, very unattractive to school administrators as they seek to employ teachers.

Whether the interview is satisfactory in terms of obtaining a position or not, it should be terminated by an expression of appreciation for the opportunity of the meeting. Within the next twenty-four hours you should send a hand-written note of thanks to the personnel director, principal, and music supervisor.

In some instances, distance prohibits the personal interview. In this case, the letters of recommendation are usually the key to job placement. Maintaining contact with your references and your evidenced appreciation for their time in writing letters on your behalf are of extreme importance to your future professional success.

Professional Organizations

Your membership in the college student chapter of professional organizations such as Music Educators National Conference is an asset in obtaining a teaching position. Interest in these groups is one evidence of your desire for continued professional growth.

As you approach your first year of full-time teaching, you may be given the opportunity (or required) to join several teacher groups. Depending upon your specialization you will choose from the following: Music Educators National Conference and the state affiliated organization, American String Teachers Association, National School Orchestra Association, American Choral Directors Association, American Bandmasters Association, Music Teachers National Association, the local music teachers association, National Education Association, classroom teachers association, and the local faculty club.

You will naturally wish to associate yourself with music groups. However, your membership in general education organizations such as National Education Association is desirable for several reasons:

1. You become acquainted with the goals of general education.
2. You are informed of new techniques in general education.
3. You give evidence of your interest in the total education of children.
4. You become involved professionally and socially with other faculty members.

As has been emphasized throughout this book, professional growth is continuous. Your membership and active participation in professional organizations offer you the opportunity to build an exciting career as a music teacher.

Summation

Each of the subjects discussed in the preceding pages is unique in its contribution to the development of the music department and to your growth in student teaching. You will find that a balance between effective organizational procedures and dynamic teaching is essential to the promotion of the school music department.

Suggestions For Further Reading

A Career in Music Education, *Music Educators National Conference, 1962.*

Glenn, Neal E., and Edgar M. Turrentine, Introduction to Advanced Study in Music Education. *Dubuque, Iowa: William C. Brown Company, 1968, p. 87.*

Rich, Alan, Careers and Opportunities in Music. *New York: E. P. Dutton, & Co., Inc., 1964.*

Sur, William R., and Charles F. Schuller, Music Education for Teen-Agers. *New York: Harper & Row, Publishers, 1966, Chapters 14 and 15.*

Appendix:
Evaluation Forms

Student Teaching Self-Evaluation Scale

Name_____Date _____

Directions: Read each item carefully and check the answer which is most descriptive of your experience in student teaching. Use the space provided between items to explain your answer or to formulate your own answer if needed. If you cannot determine the answer consult with your college supervisor. In case the item is not applicable to your student teaching situation, please explain why.

1. Which of the following most nearly describes the procedure which you followed in reporting to your student teaching assignment?

   a. reported directly to cooperating teacher on or after the day when campus classes began at (college).
   b. reported to principal's office on or after the day when campus classes began at (college).
   c. made an appointment and called on principal and cooperating teacher on first day of classes at (college).
   d. made an appointment and conferred with principal and cooperating teacher in advance of the first day of classes on the campus.

2. When did you actually begin your student teaching?

   a. after the semester's classes had begun.
   b. on the first day of classes.
   c. between the time the public school's semester started and the first day of classes.
   d. on the first day of the semester in the school to which assigned.

3. How many times have you reported late to your student teaching assignment?

   a. 5 or more
   b. 3-4
   c. 1-2
   d. none

4. How many days have you been absent from your student teaching assignment?

   a. 5 or more
   b. 3-4
   c. 1-2
   d. none

5. When your cooperating teacher notified you in advance to be prepared to teach on a subsequent date, what type of lesson planning did you do?

95

a. waited for the cooperating teacher to tell you what to do.
b. thought through a plan to follow but did not put plan in writing.
c. sketched lesson plans.
d. prepared complete written lesson plans.

6. What did you do when you made preparation to teach a lesson?

a. decided how to present the lesson without the counsel of the cooperating teacher.
b. briefly discussed or presented sketchy lesson plans to the cooperating teacher for approval.
c. usually presented complete lesson plans to cooperating teacher for his suggestions and approval.
d. always presented complete lesson plans to cooperating teacher for his suggestions and approval.

7. In preparing to teach your early lessons, did you seek assistance from your college supervisor?

a. did not ask college supervisor for assistance.
b. briefly discussed idea for a lesson.
c. presented a sketch of lesson (rehearsal) plan to the college supervisor.
d. presented the complete lesson (rehearsal) plan to the college supervisor for his approval.

8. How often during the semester have you had sole responsibility for conducting a class with the teacher in the room?

a. 0-5 class periods
b. 6-10 class periods
c. 11-20 class periods
d. 21 or more class periods

9. How many days have you taught the same class in succession?

a. 2-3
b. 4-6
c. 7-10
d. 11 or more

10. Which of the following best describes your student teaching experience in planning and teaching a unit in general music?

a. did not plan or teach a unit.
b. did not plan but taught a unit planned by the cooperating teacher.
c. planned a unit in cooperation with the teacher and taught it.
d. planned a unit which was approved by the cooperating teacher and taught it.

11. For how many different levels of general music classes have you had complete responsibility for at least five periods?

    a. 1
    b. 2
    c. 3
    d. 4

12. For how many different training groups (choir, band, orchestra) have you had complete responsibility for at least five periods?

    a. 1
    b. 2
    c. 3
    d. 4

13. For how many different performing groups (choir, band, orchestra) have you had complete responsibility for at least five periods?

    a. 0
    b. 1
    c. 2
    d. 3

14. Which of the following best describes your success in maintaining classroom control?

    a. the class was usually attentive during the instructional period.
    b. the class was occasionally attentive during the instructional period.
    c. the class was seldom attentive during the instructional period.
    d. the class was never attentive during the instructional period.

15. How did your success in maintaining classroom control compare with that of the cooperating teacher?

    a. not nearly as good as the cooperating teacher.
    b. nearly as good as the cooperating teacher.
    c. as good as the cooperating teacher.
    d. better than the cooperating teacher.

16. How do you rate yourself as a conductor?

    a. experienced frustration.
    b. had a few experiences of success.
    c. had more success with training group than with advanced group.
    d. experienced feeling of success in directing.

17. Which of the following best describes your experience in counseling and working with individual students?

a. had no opportunity to work with individual pupils.
b. seldom counseled or worked with individual pupils.
c. occasionally counseled or worked with individual pupils.
d. frequently counseled and worked with pupils with learning and other types of problems.

18. Which of the following best describes your student teaching experience with regard to school assemblies?

a. never attended an assembly.
b. attended one or more assemblies,
c. assisted teacher in planning assembly programs.
d. was in charge of preparation of assembly program.

19. Which of the following best describes your student teaching experience with regard to P.T.A. meetings?

a. never attended any P.T.A. meetings.
b. attended one P.T.A. meeting.
c. attended two P.T.A. meetings.
d. attended all P.T.A. meetings.

20. Which of the following best describes your student teaching experience with regard to school sponsored clubs or organizations?

a. did not observe or otherwise have connection with a club.
b. occasionally observed a club meeting.
c. regularly observed a club meeting,
d. served as an assistant or regular club sponsor.

21. Which of the following best describes your student teaching experience with regard to meeting parents of students?

a. never met any parents of the students.
b. met one or two parents of students.
c. met three to five parents of students.
d. met six or more parents of students.

22. Which of the following best describes your student teaching experience with regard to home-room meetings?

a. did not observe a home-room.
b. observed a home-room occasionally.
c. observed a home-room regularly.
d. observed and assisted with a home-room regularly.

23. Which of the following best describes your student teaching experience with regard to faculty meetings?

a. did not attend a faculty meeting.

b. attended one faculty meeting.

c. attended two or more faculty meetings.

d. attended faculty meetings regularly.

24. How many times did you eat lunch in the school lunchroom?

a. none

b. 1-3

c. 4-10

d. 11 or more

25. Which of the following best describes your student teaching experience in regard to consulting with the school counselor?

a. did not consult with counselor.

b. had one conference with counselor.

c. had two or three conferences with counselor.

d. had four or more conferences with counselor.

26. Did you make use of the cumulative records of the students in your classes?

a. did not examine any cumulative records.

b. examined the cumulative records of some of the students.

c. examined the cumulative records of most of the students.

d. examined the cumulative records of all of the students.

27. Which of the following best describes your student teaching experience with regard to talking and conferring with the principal?

a. had no occasion to confer with principal other than speaking to him in the hall.

b. had from one to four informal chats or conferences with principal after the initial conference.

c. had five or more informal chats or conferences with principal after the initial conference.

d. had numerous informal chats or conferences with principal, and he observed me teach on one or more occasions.

28. How much experience did you receive with regard to grading tests?

a. did not grade any test papers.

b. graded one set of test papers.

c. graded 2-4 sets of test papers.

d. graded 5 or more sets of test papers.

29. How much experience did you receive in making out tests?

a. did not make out any tests.

b. made out 1 or 2 tests.

c. made out 3 or 4 tests.

d. made out 5 or more tests.

30. How much experience did you receive in determining the six weeks' grades of the students?

    a. did not have an opportunity to assist with or make out grades.
    b. was shown the system for determining final grades.
    c. gave the cooperating teacher some assistance in making out final grades.
    d. was given practically complete responsibility for making out final grades.

31. Which of the following best describes your student teaching experience in securing instructional materials?

    a. did not secure materials other than those provided by the cooperating teacher.
    b. obtained some materials for my own use other than those provided by the cooperating teacher.
    c. obtained some materials for use by the students and teacher.
    d. obtained much material for use by the students and teacher.

32. Which best describes your use of the college supervisor as a resource person in securing materials and other assistance?

    a. did not ask college supervisor for materials or assistance.
    b. asked for and received materials one time.
    c. asked but received no response from college supervisor.
    d. asked for and received satisfactory assistance from the college supervisor on several occasions.

33. Which of the following best describes your willingness to volunteer for extra work in connection with your student teaching assignment?

    a. did not volunteer for extra work.
    b. seldom volunteered for extra work.
    c. frequently volunteered for extra work.
    d. frequently volunteered and even requested that you be permitted to do additional work.

34. Which of the following best describes how well you cooperated with your cooperating teacher in your student teaching term?

    a. made little effort to cooperate with cooperating teacher.
    b. made some effort to cooperate with cooperating teacher.
    c. made a reasonable effort to cooperate with cooperating teacher.
    d. made a great effort to cooperate with cooperating teacher.

35. Which of the following best describes your relationship with the cooperating teacher?

   a. poor working relationship with cooperating teacher.
   b. fairly satisfactory working relationship with cooperating teacher.
   c. good working relationship with cooperating teacher.
   d. excellent working relationship with cooperating teacher.

36. How frequently did you report to your college supervisor for consultation?

   a. only when requested by the supervisor.
   b. after each visit by supervisor.
   c. after each visit by supervisor and on several other occasions.
   d. regularly each week.

37. How effective do you believe your teaching was with regard to pupil achievement?

   a. relatively ineffective
   b. slightly effective
   c. moderately effective
   d. exceptionally effective

38. How do you evaluate the desirability of your over-all student teaching assignment?

   a. undesirable
   b. barely satisfactory
   c. satisfactory
   d. highly desirable

Please list, describe, or otherwise indicate the most satisfactory aspects of your student teaching experience.

Please list, describe, or otherwise indicate the least satisfactory aspects of your student teaching experience, and indicate how the program could be improved.

Evaluation of Student Teaching in Music

(For Cooperating Teacher and College Supervisor)

Please check the appropriate column following applicable items.

	Outstanding	Superior	Average	Poor	Unsatisfactory
PERSONAL QUALITIES					
Dress and neatness					
General health and vitality					
Voice					
Maturity and emotional stability					
Patience with and friendliness toward students					
Initiative					
Punctuality and regularity in attendance					
PROFESSIONAL ATTRIBUTES					
Poise, courtesy, and tactfulness					
Ingenuity and resourcefulness					
Attitude toward students					
Cooperativeness with cooperating teacher					
Cooperativeness with college supervisor					
Ability to maintain discipline					
Understanding of students					
Interest in teaching					

TEACHING METHODOLOGY

Preparation for rehearsals and classes
Skill in presentation
Care and use of instructional materials
Attention to individual differences
Command of a variety of teaching procedures
General understanding of principles of learning
Attention to physical aspects of classroom

COMMAND OF SUBJECT MATTER

Knowledge of music
Ability to project knowledge to students
Ability to maintain students' interest
Ability to inspire maximum effort from students
Ability to evaluate the results of learning

PREDICTION OF SUCCESS AS A TEACHER

Weakness:

Strength:

Other comments:

Semester Report of Student Teaching Record

University of Texas
Department of Music

Student Teacher's Name _____ Date _____

Record number in blanks as follows: 1 superior, 2 good, 3 average, 4 fair, 5 poor

Musical Ability: Voice _____ Piano _____ Conducting _____
Rhythm _____ General Musicianship _____
Sight Reading _____

Average
( )

Teaching Ability: General Instruction _____ Organization of
materials _____ Subject matter _____ Patience _____ Selection
of materials _____ Planning _____ Methods _____ Discipline _____
Attention to lighting _____ Ventilation _____ Equipment _____
Condition of room _____ Use of audio-visual techniques _____
and other _____ Special interests _____ Class attention and
interest _____ Vocabulary _____

Average
( )

Conducting Ability: Attack _____ Down-beat _____ Up-beat _____
Cues _____ Release _____ Tempo Changes _____ Divided
beats _____ Left hand _____ Interpretation _____ Knowledge
of score _____ Facial expression _____ Precision _____
Flexibility _____ Intonation _____

Average
( )

Personal Attributes: Health: _____ Vitality _____ Adaptability _____
Tact _____ Culture _____ Scholarship _____ Poise _____
Interest _____ Cooperation _____ Loyalty _____ Leadership _____
Appearance _____ Judgment _____ Initiative _____
Personality _____ Attendance _____ Punctuality _____
Organization _____ Humor _____ Enthusiasm _____
Posture _____

Average
( )

Adaptability to school community: Attendance at P.T.A. _____
Cooperation with student performances _____ Relationship with
principal _____ Relationship with other teachers _____
Relationship with parents _____

Average
( )

Negative Idiosyncracies (i.e., talks too much)

_____
_____
_____   Cooperating teacher _____
                                                     School _____
Additional Comments:
_____   Class (i.e. Band III) _____
_____

Reprinted by permission of Charlotte DuBois, Professor of Music and Education, University of Texas.

Southern Methodist University
Evaluation of Student Teaching in Music
(To be completed by cooperating teacher)

Name of Student Teacher _____Date _____

CHARACTERISTICS AFFECTING TEACHING SUCCESS

Directions: Check the appropriate position on each scale. Underline strong points. Encircle weak points.

Superior   Average   Inferior

1. CLASSROOM PERSONALITY
Is mentally alert; has sense of humor; exercises self-control; has drive and vitality; is poised and confident; is cheerful. | | | | | | | | | | |

2. PERSONAL APPEARANCE
Exhibits good taste and neatness in dress; is clean; has no distracting mannerisms. | | | | | | | | | | |

3. SOCIAL QUALITIES
Is friendly, understanding and helpful, is courteous and tactful; is interested in pupils; has ability to get along with others and understand their problems. | | | | | | | | | | |

4. LOYALTY AND COOPERATION
Is willing and able to take suggestions and criticisms; cooperates with associates and supervisors; upholds school policies. | | | | | | | | | | |

5. PROFESSIONAL ZEAL
Is interested in teaching; takes steps toward self-improvement; is an enthusiastic worker; believes that teaching is worthwhile. | | | | | | | | | | |

6. KNOWLEDGE OF SUBJECT MATTER IN MUSIC TEACHING FIELD
Has an understanding and a working knowledge of content; has adequate theoretical knowledge, keyboard knowledge, conducting skill, background in music history and literature, and performance skills adequate for teaching assignment. | | | | | | | | | | |

7. ABILITY TO ORGANIZE MATERIALS FOR TEACHING PURPOSES
Makes adequate plans for teaching; selects materials with due regard for individual differences; organizes materials effectively. | | | | | | | | | | |

8. ABILITY TO ORGANIZE LEARNING SITUATIONS
Has general mastery of method; is able to create effective learning situations; obtains wide pupil participation; maintains proper balance between teacher-pupil activity; provides for individual differences. | | | | | | | | | | |

9. CLASS ACHIEVEMENT
   Achieves his objectives in the light of pupil abilities; selects appropriate appraisal techniques. |||||||||

10. CLASSROOM MANAGEMENT AND DISCIPLINE
    Is fair and just in dealing with pupils; secures good working conditions; understands pupils and their needs; is concerned for the physical welfare of pupils; has the interest and cooperation of pupils; develops social responsibility in pupils. |||||||||

11. VOICE AND SPEECH
    Is clear and distinct; has good inflection and modulation; is easy to understand; uses correct pronunciation; is free from irritating mannerisms. |||||||||

12. USE OF ORAL AND WRITTEN ENGLISH
    Has ability to present ideas simply and clearly; uses good English in and out of classroom. |||||||||

IMPORTANT:

Supplement the above rating with a statement covering any additional points. Make note of any characteristics or abilities that particularly qualify or disqualify the individual for teaching.

Signed_____ Cooperating teacher in_____
                                                          School

Student Teaching Evaluation Form

College of Education
Michigan State University

STUDENT _____

SUPERVISOR _____

This completed form is to be given to the student at the end of the term.

	Optional	Mid-Term	Optional	Final Week
I. WORKING WITH PEOPLE				
1. Maintains reasonable level of expectations from pupils.				
2. Retains adult status while working at pupil's level.				
3. Gains confidence and respect of pupils.				
4. Works successfully with pupils of various backgrounds.				
5. Relates with staff members in a comfortable manner.				
6. Seeks and uses suggestions from staff and administration.				

7. Seeks opportunity to meet and talk with parents at PTA, etc.

8. Meets parents at mature and professional level.

9. Communicates effectively with parents.

Specific activities in the area of Working With People that merit continuation:

Optional

Mid-Term

Optional

Final

Specific activities that would probably bring about improvement in the area of Working With People:

Optional

Mid-Term

Optional

Final

	Optional	Mid-Term	Optional	Final Week

II. ESTABLISHING CLASSROOM CLIMATE AND MANAGING INSTRUCTION

1. Assists pupils in developing habits of democratic living.

2. Handles discipline problems effectively.

3. Permissive and authorative manner is appropriately adjusted to classroom situation.

4. Demonstrates that he is judicious and fair with all pupils.

5. Provides for group discussion and pupil participation. Involves pupils in appropriate decision making situations.

6. Works in such a manner that individual pupils seek his help with personal problems.

7. Moves to specific learning activities as group shows readiness.

8. Paces activities so that interest lag among pupils is minimized.

9. Uses methods designed to reach and maintain attention of all pupils.

10. Arranges and provides for facilities in the classroom conductive to optimum learning (chairs, tables, library corners, bulletin boards, etc.)

11. Adjusts pupil activity (neatness, orderliness and quietness) to the instructional situation.

12. Attends to factors of ventilation, temperature, and lighting in the classroom.

13. Considers and attends to factors related to pupil safety.

	Optional	Mid-Term	Optional	Final Week
14. Makes assignments so that pupils clearly understand what is to be done, and why it is to be done.				
15. Introduces and implements daily plans meaningfully.				
16. Uses a variety of teaching techniques.				
17. Uses wisely a variety of audio-visual aids and supplementary materials.				
18. Teaches planned units effectively.				
19. Daily instruction is directed and managed so that pupils are interested, motivated, and show a desire to learn.				
20. Explanations are logical; uses types of reasoning appropriate to pupil level.				
21. Works effectively with pupils in small groups.				
22. Works effectively with pupils in large groups (entire class).				

23. Develops a questioning attitude and intellectual curiosity in pupils.

24. Develops effective processes of problem solving and critical thinking on the part of pupils.

25. Evidences awareness of interest and attention span of pupils.

26. Recognizes the need for re-teaching at appropriate intervals.

27. Deals appropriately with unexpected situations as they develop.

28. Shows ability to use smoothly spontaneous situations to achieve aims.

29. Adapts instruction to changing needs of pupils and class.

Specific activities in the area of Establishing Classroom Climate and Managing Instruction:

Optional

Mid-Term

Optional

Final

Specific activities that would probably bring about improvement in the area of Establishing Classroom Climate and Managing Instruction:

Optional

Mid-Term

Optional

Final

	Optional	Mid-Term	Optional	Final Week

III. PLANNING FOR INSTRUCTION

1. Shows evidence of consistent reading, study, and time spent on gathering information for his teaching plans.

2. His plans demonstrate recognition of appropriate use of textbook.

3. Selects appropriate teaching materials and has them available for use.

4. His plans for short-term (daily) and long-term (unit or project) work are thorough.

5. His plans show that he considers sequence and continuity of pupil experiences as key factors in learning.

6. When suitable, plans for a field trip and/or use of community resources in his teaching.

7. Plans reveal a wide variety of teaching techniques.

114

	Optional	Mid-Term	Optional	Final Week
8. Studies individual pupil and school records carefully as a basis for evaluating pupil progress.				
9. Recognizes individual differences in evaluating pupil performance.				
10. Uses a wide variety of procedures for appraising pupil performance.				
11. Grades which he has given are arrived at fairly and are related appropriately to acceptable criteria of good evaluation.				
12. Recognizes the importance of parent-teacher conferences in evaluation.				
13. Evaluation is made in terms of the purposes of the subject or grade taught.				

Specific activities in the area of Planning for Instruction that merit continuation:

Optional

Mid-Term

Optional

Final

Specific activities that would probably bring about improvement in the area of Planning for Instruction:

Optional

Mid-Term

Optional

Final

	Optional	Mid-Term	Optional	Final Week
IV. COMMAND OF SUBJECT AND TEACHING MATERIALS				
1. Is ably prepared in the subjects and/or grades he is assigned to teach.				
2. Has shown persistence in seeking added information and knowledge from many sources in his teaching subjects this term.				
3. Has sought help and suggestions from specialists and consultants in subject areas where needed.				
4. Has knowledge of a variety of teaching materials in his subject and/or grade.				
5. Is able to relate his area of knowledge to other areas of knowledge.				

Specific activities in the area of Command of Subject and Teaching Materials that merit continuation:

Optional

117

Mid-Term

Optional

Final

Specific activities that would probably bring about improvement in the area of Command of Subject and Teaching Materials:

Optional

Mid-Term

Optional

Final

	Optional	Mid-Term	Optional	Final Week
V. PERSONAL QUALITIES AND PROFESSIONAL QUALITIES				
1. Is rarely absent because of illness.				
2. Stamina adequate for the job of teaching.				
3. Shows physical vitality and enthusiasm.				
4. Appears to be emotionally stable.				
5. Tends toward flexibility rather than rigidity in thought and behavior patterns.				
6. Has an appropriate sense of humor.				
7. Dresses appropriately.				
8. Always neat and well groomed.				
9. Seldom if ever late.				

119

10. Carries out all tasks effectively and on time.

11. Trustworthy in all respects.

12. Accepts and profits from constructive criticism.

13. Demonstrates ability for self-evaluation.

14. Reveals genuine interest in pupils.

15. Sensitive to feelings and needs of others.

16. Adjusts voice appropriately to the instructional situation.

17. Uses spoken language correctly and effectively.

18. Writes effectively and legibly.

19. Spells correctly.

20. Participates willingly in school and faculty activities.

	Optional	Mid-Term	Optional	Final Week
21. Seeks opportunity to assume responsibility.				
22. Shows interest in and helps supervise pupils in extra-class activities.				
23. Shows persistence in completion of tasks.				
24. Behaves in ethical and professional manner.				
25. Indicates a sincere enthusiasm for the job.				

Specific activities in the area of Personal and Professional Qualities that merit continuation:

Optional

Mid-Term

121

Optional

Final

Specific activities that would probably bring about improvement in the area of **Personal and Professional Qualities:**

Optional

Mid-Term

Optional

Final

Reprinted by permission of the College of Education, Michigan State University.

Bibliography

Andrews, Frances M., "Guideposts for Beginning Teachers," Music Educators Journal, LIV, No. 2 (1967).

———, and Joseph A. Leeder, Guiding Junior High School Pupils in Music Experiences. Englewood Cliffs, N.J.: Prentice-Hall, Inc., 1963.

Benson, Earl C., "Modular Scheduling in Music," Music Educators Journal, LIV, No. 4 (1967), 55-66.

Berg, Herman, "Conductors Corner–Use the Face, Body and Left Hand," The Instrumentalist, XXII No. 9 (1968) 74-77.

A Career in Music Education, Music Educators National Conference, 1962.

Cheyette, Irving, and Herbert Cheyette, Teaching Music Creatively in the Elementary School. New York: McGraw-Hill Book Company, 1969.

Cooper, Irvin, and Karl O. Kuersteiner, Teaching Junior High School Music Boston: Allyn & Bacon, Inc., 1967.

Dearborn, Norman, "String Tuning and Pegs," The Instrumentalist, XXIII, No. 1 (1968), 81-85.

Decker, Harold A., "Choosing Music for Performance," Choral Director's Guide, eds. Kenneth L. Neidig and John W. Jennings. West Nyack, N.Y.: Parker Publishing Co., Inc., 1967.

Dello Joio, Norman, et al, "The Contemporary Music Project for Creativity in Music Education," Music Educators Journal, LIV, No. 7 (1968), 41-72.

Diercks, Louis, "Public Relations," Choral Director's Guide, eds. Kenneth L. Neidig and John W. Jennings. West Nyack, N.Y.: Parker Publishing Co., Inc. 1967.

Douglass, C. William, "Arturo Toscanini, The Maestro of Us All," Music Educators Journal, LIV, No. 6 (1968), 69-71.

Douglass, C. William, "Chamber Music for the Musically Gifted," Music Educators Journal, LIII, No. 5 (1967), 95.

Dunlop, Richard S., *"Toward Improved Professional Practice Under Flexible Modular Scheduling,"* Journal of Teacher Education, *XIX, No. 2 (1968), 159.*

Duvall, W. Clyde, The High School Band Director's Handbook. *Englewood Cliffs, N.J.: Prentice-Hall, Inc., 1962.*

Draper, Dallas, *"Contest and Festivals,"* Choral Director's Guide, eds. *Kenneth L. Neidig and John W. Jennings. West Nyack, N.Y.: Parker Publishing Co., Inc., 1967.*

Edwards, William, *"The Recruitment of Beginners,"* The Instrumentalist, *XXIII, No. 2 (1968), 48-49.*

Ehmann, Wilhelm, Choral Directing. *Minneapolis, Minn.: Augsburg Publishing House, 1968.*

Ernst, Karl D., and Charles L. Gary, Music in General Education, *Music Educators National Conference, 1965.*

———, The Study of Music in the Elementary School: A Conceptual Approach, *Music Educators National Conference, 1967.*

Gaines, Joan, Approaches to Public Relations for the Music Educator, *Washington, D.C.: Music Educators National Conference, 1968.*

———, *"Secondary Principals Comment on Music,"* Music Educators Journal, *LIV, No. 8 (1968), 85-86.*

Galamian, Ivan, Principles of Violin Playing and Teaching. *Englewood Cliffs, N.J.: Prentice-Hall, Inc., 1962.*

Garretson, Robert L., Conducting Choral Music. *Boston: Allyn & Bacon, Inc., 1963.*

Goldman, Richard Franko, The Wind Band: Its Literature and Technique. *Boston: Allyn & Bacon, Inc., 1961.*

Graham, Floyd Freeman, Public Relations in Music Education. *New York: Exposition Press, 1954.*

Green, Elizabeth A.H., The Modern Conductor *(2nd ed.). Englewood Cliffs, N.J.: Prentice-Hall Inc., 1969.*

Hipple, Walter J., Jr. *"Humanities in the Secondary School,"* Music Educators Journal, *LIV' No. 6 (1968), 85-88, 155-61.*

Hoffer, Charles R., *"Teaching Useful Knowledge in Rehearsal,"* Music Educators Journal, *LII, No. 5 (1966), 49-51, 90-94.*

House, Robert W., Instrumental Music in Today's Schools. *Englewood Cliffs, N.J.: Prentice-Hall Inc., 1964.*

———, *"Developing an Educative Setting for Performing Groups,"* Music Educators Journal, *LIII, No. 1 (1966), 54-56, 144-49.*

Ivy, James, *"Come Blow Your Horn—An Invitation,"* The Instrumentalist, *XXIII, No. 2 (1968), 49-50.*

Knauf, Robert, "Junior High School–The Pivotal Point," Choral Director's Guide, *eds. Kenneth L. Neidig and John W. Jennings. West Nyack, N.Y.: Parker Publishing Co., Inc., 1967.*

Kuhn, Wolfgang, "Microteaching," Music Educators Journal, *LV, No. 4 (1968) 49-53.*

–––, Instrumental Music. *Allyn & Bacon, Inc., Boston, 1962.*

Larson, Le Roy, "More Than Performance: It Can Be Done," Music Educators Journal, *February, 1969, 41.*

Lawson, Warner, "Practical Rehearsal Techniques," Choral Director's Guide, *eds. Kenneth L. Neidig and John W. Jennings. West Nyack, N.Y.: Parker Publishing Co., Inc., 1967.*

Leeder, Joseph A., and William S. Haynie, Music Education in the High School. *Englewood Cliffs, N.J.: Prentice-Hall, Inc., 1964.*

Lehman, Paul R., Tests and Measurements in Music. *Englewood Cliffs, N.J.:Prentice-Hall, Inc., 1968.*

Leonhard, Charles, and Robert W. House, Foundations and Principles of Music Education. *New York: McGraw-Hill Book Company, 1959.*

Levy, Edward, "To Analyze Music, Sketch It," Music Educators Journal, *LV, No. 5 (1969), 39-40, 117-18.*

Lukin, Laszlo, "The Teaching of Singing and Music in Primary and Secondary School," Musical Education in Hungary, *ed. Frigges Sandor. Budapest: Cowina Press, 1966.*

Maslow, Abraham H., "Music Education and Peak Experiences," Music Educators Journal, *LIV, No. 6 (1968), 73-75, 163-71.*

Matchett, Robert, "Warm up Correctly for a Better Band," The Instrumentalist, *XXIII, No. 1 (1968), 70-72.*

McElheran, Brock, Conducting Technique. *New York: Oxford University Press, Inc., 1966.*

McQuerrey, Lawrence H. "Microrehearsal," Music Educators Journal, *LV, No. 4 (1968), 48-53.*

Monsour, Sally, Marilyn Cohen, and Patricia Lindell, Rhythms in Music and Dance for Children. *Belmont. California: Wadsworth Publishing Co., 1966.*

Nordholm, Harriet, Singing in the Elementary Schools. *Englewood Cliffs, N.J.: Prentice-Hall, Inc., 1966, pp. 77-79.*

Olson, Rees G. "Teaching Music Concepts by the Discovery Method," Music Educators Journal. *LIV, No. 1 (1967), 51-53, 123-31.*

Orff, Carl, and Gunild Keetman, Music for Children. *New York: Schott Music Corp., 1960.*

Pfautsch, Lloyd, Mental Warmups for the Choral Conductor, *New York: Lawson-Gould, 1969.*

Price, Gertrude, "Improvisation in the Elementary Classroom," Music Educators Journal, *LIV, No. 8 (1968), 42-47.*

Purrington, Bruce R., "Team Teaching in the Musical Arts," Music Educators Journal, *LIII, No. 8 (1967), 135-37.*

Reimer, Bennett, "Curriculum Reforms and the Junior High General Music Class," Music Educators Journal, *LIII, No. 2 (1966), 42-44, 123-27.*

———, *"Performance and Aesthetic Sensitivity,"* Music Educators Journal *(1968), 27-29, 107-14. .*

Rich, Alan, Careers and Opportunities in Music. *New York: E. P. Dutton & Co., Inc., 1964.*

Roberts, Charles, "Flexible Modular Scheduling and Instrumental Music," The Instrumentalist, *XXIV, No. 1 (1968), 77-78.*

Russell-Smith, Geoffrey, "Introducing Kodaly Principles into Elementary Teaching," Music Educators Journal, *LIV, No. 3 (1967), 43-45.*

Sur, William Raymond, and Charles Francis Schuller, Music Education for Teen-Agers. *N.Y.: Harper & Row, Publishers, 1958.*

Thomson, William, "The Ensemble Director and Musical Concepts," Music Educators Journal, *LIV, No. 9 (1968), 44-46.*

Turrentine, Edgar M. and Neal E., Introduction to Advanced Study in Music Education. *Dubuque, Iowa: William C. Brown Company, 1968.*

Verrastro, Ralph E. "Improving Student-Teacher Supervision," Music Educators Journal, *LIV, No. 3 (1967), 81-83.*

Weerts, Richard, "The Beginning Instrumental Program in Perspective," The Instrumentalist, *XXIII, No. 2 (1968), 46-47.*

Index